POEMS FROM MAINE

TAKE HEART

THE COMPLETE COLLECTION

Edited by Wesley McNair

Down East Books

Down East Books

Published by Down East Books
An imprint of Globe Pequot
Trade division of The Rowman & Littlefield Publishing Group, Inc.
4501 Forbes Blvd., Ste. 200
Lanham, MD 20706
www.rowman.com
www.downeastbooks.com

Distributed by NATIONAL BOOK NETWORK

ISBN 978-1-68475-065-8 (paperback)
ISBN 978-1-68475-080-1 (e-book)

Library of Congress Cataloging-in-Publication Data

Names: McNair, Wesley, editor.
Title: Take heart : poems from Maine : the complete collection / edited by Wesley McNair.
Description: Paperback edition. | Lanham, MD : Down East Books, [2022]
Identifiers: LCCN 2022025408 (print) | LCCN 2022025409 (ebook) | ISBN 9781684750658 (paperback ; alk. paper) | ISBN 9781684750801 (epub)
Subjects: LCSH: American poetry--Maine. | Maine--Poetry. | LCGFT: Poetry.
Classification: LCC PS548.M2 T35 2022 (print) | LCC PS548.M2 (ebook) | DDC 811.008/09741--dc23
LC record available at https://lccn.loc.gov/2022025408
LC ebook record available at https://lccn.loc.gov/2022025409

British Library Cataloguing in Publication Information available

The paper used in this publication meets the minimum requirements of American National Standard for Information Sciences—Permanence of Paper for Printed Library Materials, ANSI/NISO Z39.48-1992.

For Joshua Bodwell, Gibson Fay-LeBlanc,
David Turner, and Hannah Perry

CONTENTS

2. The Place Inside the Place

3. Changes of Heart

4. The World and Back Again

7. A Journey of One

INTRODUCTION

If we had set out to create a program that was more threatening to the connection between poetry and its audience, we could hardly have done better than the system we have in America today. Poetry books are routinely printed in runs of less than a thousand copies, and only a few are given reviews or shelfspace in bookstores. Partly in self-defense, poets band together in groups or aesthetic schools and offer bookstore readings attended by fellow poets and a few of the like-minded, or university readings attended mostly by students pressed into service. Meanwhile the general public, standing at the edges of such events, decides that today's poetry is probably not for them.

Yet people outside of literary circles continue to value poetry. They understand the poem's unique power to express in a few words the feelings that matter most to us. That is why they turn to poetry on milestone occasions like weddings and funerals and commencement exercises. It was my mission as Maine Poet Laureate to find new ways of bringing poetry to the people, reminding them in the process that it is not only for special occasions, but for every day of our lives.

So, with the help of the Maine Writers and Publishers Alliance, I edited and introduced for five years a weekly column for Maine newspapers called *Take Heart: A Conversation in Poetry*, making it my first initiative. Each week, *Take Heart* featured a previously published poem by one of our state's poets, some from the past and most from the present. *Take Heart* appeared in thirty newspapers and newsletters across the state, with a combined circulation of well over 250,000 readers.

The responses to *Take Heart* came from all quarters. I received thanks by email from both the poets whose work was reprinted and readers who were affected by it. Scores of the column's poems were mailed and emailed in the enthusiasm of discovery. They were displayed in grade schools and used for high school and prison classes in creative writing. A full set was copied to help a man fighting an extreme form of dementia learn once again how to read.

I am of course pleased by the popularity of the column, but no less pleased by the visibility it has given Maine's poets, proving both the relevance of figures long gone from the literary scene and the quality and diversity of our current writing. Who knew there were so many good poems being written in our state? How many other states could match such a production? When I started the initiative, I hoped to bring poetry to the people of Maine. I am proud to have brought them *this* poetry, and these poets, whose best work richly deserves a wide readership.

This anthology collects all the poetry from the *Take Heart* initiative begun in May 2011 and originally published in two hardcover volumes — poems about wishes, pleasures, and sorrows; poems about familiar experiences we only thought we knew; poems that will inspire tears and laughter and help us to carry on. I offer them with thanks to Joshua Bodwell and Gibson Fay-LeBlanc, directors of MWPA and partners in the laureateship; David Turner and Hannah Perry, my special MWPA assistants for the *Take Heart* column; Michael Steere, my editor at Down East Books; and the poets of Maine, whose unique and astonishing vision this book celebrates. Their poems entertained and instructed Maine readers over the five years of the *Take Heart* column. Now their inspiration will continue, throughout Maine and across the country.

Wesley McNair
Mercer, Maine

1

Heart Faces

Mr. Fix-It

Stuart Kestenbaum

My father never made anything or
fixed anything, even though we had
the obligatory tools in the basement,

to my great grandfather the carpenter,
the once-used brushes and the mysterious
cans of paint and shellac. And he never
cooked anything either, never turned

the coffee pot down to perk,
never cracked an egg and only once
that I remember barbecued steaks,
the smoke rising to heaven like a burnt offering

from the charred remains. When he returned
home at night, the smell of gas and oil
still close to his clothes, he'd settle on the couch
finishing a New York Times crossword puzzle while

keeping track of the Yankees on TV, until he
fell asleep, only to rouse when I'd change the channel.
"I was watching that," he'd mumble, though asleep,
and I'd believe him, but now I think he wasn't there

but had been at his domestic work, the night shift,
dreaming the lives of his children,
building a house of words, writing
the perfect story whose ending we never get to.

Peaches

Kate Barnes

Jenny, because you are twenty-three
        (and my daughter),
you think you know everything;
and because I am fifty-three
                                (and your mother),
I think *I* know everything.
A week ago you picked up two green little peaches,
only half-grown and still hard,
from under the loaded peach tree
and put them on the kitchen window sill;
and I thought
        (though I didn't say a word):
they're too small, they will just rot
but I won't move them, Jenny put them there.

Now the summer is over and you are gone,
the mornings are cool, squashes conquer the garden,
the tree swallows have flown away, crickets sing —
and the sweet juice of your peaches runs down my chin.

Spaghetti Western Days

Annie Farnsworth

for Jacob

My son, just turned five
has not learned the rules about wild versus tame.
Always busy, transplanting field violets
and dandelions into my garden to make it
"more beautiful," smuggling toads
and millipedes into the house to keep for pets.
I mourn those small lives whose tiny,
dessicated remains I must chip from the windowsills,
shake from shoeboxes, and I try to explain
why we must leave nature where it is.

But this is a boy who snitches
my scotch tape and writing paper
to roll his own "cigarettes," who knows
that the good guys wear white hats
but he wants a black one anyway. A boy
with holsters and spurs, no horse in sight.
Days like this, when both front and back doors
flap like wings, and the big pine out back
flies a banner of kite tail,
I see that my doorstep is no boundary

and that there are frontiers I haven't yet
got eyes to see. And if I know anything,
just one damn thing worth knowing
in this lifetime, I've learned it only since
this whirlwind of a boy
blew into town.

Roses

Thomas Carper

During the night of fever, as she lay
Between an exhausted wakefulness and sleep,
I sat beside her fearfully, in dismay
When her slow breathing would become so deep
It seemed that she might slip beyond recall.
Then I would touch her; then she would revive;
Then, when her eyelids opened and a small
Smile would greet me, hope would come alive.
With morning, the ordeal was over. Gone
Was every trace of illness. A soft rain
Had swept across the countryside at dawn,
So even our garden was made fresh again.
Then Janet went among our roses where
She and the roses shone in luminous air.

Cullen: Four Days Old, Waking

Preston H. Hood

I hug my first grandson rock him back
& forth above the swaying white
daffodils,

hear his breath measured & calm,
& discover those sea-deep eyes that blink
from the water-music of sleep.

His tiny fingers open, close, embrace
my thumb, the moment sharing. Our lives
intertwine — branch toward light.

While he gazes up at me & into this world,
his eyelids flutter. I wonder what he sees, how he
thinks, what does he want to hear from me?

Four days, just four, too young
to focus or concentrate, yet somewhere
in sleep where he should be.

How irresistible in my arms: his head leaning
against my chest, the bright noon warming
around him. Peace composes his face.

His serene expression breathes love to me
in code. I hold him long enough against my cheek
to feel his pulse & yawning grin

awaken, & arouse in me a new beginning
where everything again is possible.
When I listen closely, I can almost hear him speak.

Eighty-Five

Elizabeth Tibbetts

"Shoo," she says and waves me away
like a big fly, though she's been happy to talk,
her lipsticked mouth taking me word by word
through her life: born in this town, never left,
widowed once, divorced twice, one daughter —
now dead — and forty years in the fish factory.

She and the girls loved every minute of it,
racing — piece work, you know. Gossip swooping
through the long room like a flock of starlings
while their hands, separate animals, filled
hundreds of tins day after day. Some days
they'd lift a big icy fish from the crate,

lay it on the boiler to steam, then eat it
with their fingers. There was never anything
so fresh. She fiddles with a button on her robe,
her nails roughly painted to match her mouth,
and no, she doesn't need help with her shampoo,
washing her creases, soaking her swollen feet.

She looks as though she never could get out
of that chair, but somehow it's easy
to see how she would have stood on a corner
in the South End, her feet in pumps, one hip
cocked, talking to a girlfriend, and seeming
not to notice the men from the shipyard loose
on Saturday night in their clean white shirts.

Watermelon

Susan Deborah King

In memory of Lyn Colby

There being not much of later
to enjoy it in, he suggested to me,
down-island neighbor, we cut it open
right now, the "personal-sized" melon
I brought, since he told me
I might as well take back home
the rhubarb pie I made for him in the hospital
because he preferred his fruit plain.
He could be plain in his speaking too!
Was it just the emotion of the moment
or was this the sweetest, juiciest, most rubiate
fruit a tooth ever sank into, bright
in the mouth as the July day outside
his shut in, TV-in-the-background house,
next to which sat his big red truck
with his late wife's name, same as his boat's,
emblazoned on the hood? Next to that
rose a yellow, cross-hatched
squared off mountain of idle,
due to his illness, traps. He was a strapping,
loose-jointed man, a hunter, a kidder, skipper
of any room he sauntered through.

When I got up to leave, he couldn't rise,
oxygen tubes pinched into his nostrils.
He took my hand — a surprise — looked
into my eyes and couldn't find the bottom.

1940

Sharon Bray

After they left the roller rink
and drove out of streetlight range,
he showed her Orion,
the one constellation
she still could name
into the year she died.
He could have seduced her
on the back seat blanket
of his downhill-fast Model A.
Instead he gave her one ripe orange,
which she took home to her mother.

Rained Out

Gerald George

After the Red Sox
blew their season
by losing three straight
in the playoffs to Chicago,
it rained for days.

"Coincidence," I said
over coffee down at
Archibald's One-Stop.

"Think what you like,"
Homer Jones replied,
buttoning up his slicker.
Then he walked out
and never spoke
to me again.

The Man Who Likes Cows

Sheila Gray Jordan

Thirty miles from the city,
past the first town
with a small name,
cows are in a field,
black and white Holsteins,
nudes with dairy nipples.

He stops the car,
opens the door on my side,
and I get out to see the cows
who look at us over their shoulders —
sloppy, dumb broads, wading
in milk and honeybees.

He is a man who likes cows.
But they are not to be coaxed,
cud-happy this spring day,
the grass green.
Something big — a bell or a sunset —
is necessary to move them.

Like Jove, "Speaking
their tongue. . . ," in his city suit,
he cups his hands: the Moo
rising from his groin,
a brazen klaxon,
helloing.

The call bends their thick skulls.
They lift their heads —
all eyes and ears —
coming on to crowd the fence.
I take his hand, make a fist of it
with its gold ring.

Love Is Not All: It Is Not Meat Nor Drink

Edna St. Vincent Millay

Love is not all: it is not meat nor drink
Nor slumber nor a roof against the rain,
Nor yet a floating spar to men that sink
And rise and sink and rise and sink again;
Love can not fill the thickened lung with breath,
Nor clean the blood, nor set the fractured bone;
Yet many a man is making friends with death
Even as I speak, for lack of love alone.
It well may be that in a difficult hour,
Pinned down by pain and moaning for release,
Or nagged by want past resolution's power,
I might be driven to sell your love for peace,
Or trade the memory of this night for food.
It may well be. I do not think I would.

Her Telling

Thomas R. Moore

When she told me
after she'd uncoiled the line
with the steel stakes at the ends
to set straight rows of peas
clad in her denim cover-alls
and tall rubber boots at seventy,
after she'd tossed garden stones
onto the long windrow
beyond the asparagus,
after she'd showed me
the ants climbing the peony stalks
to the hard buds and cupped hands
beside the kitchen propane tanks,
and even after years of stirring
green tomato mincemeat
on the yellow Glenwood
and tugging carrots
from the hot August soil
and snapping off ears of corn
and letting me pick clean
the tree of seckel pears —
the hard tangy red fruit —
in October,
even forty years after that Christmas day
when she smashed the third floor door,

the children listening below,
to find her husband inside,
dead by his own hand,
my grandmother was stunned
by her own telling.

Mom Gets In One of My Poems

Martin Steingesser

"I thought I missed you, darling," she is saying on the phone.
"No, you woke me. It's 7:30."
"Oh —" she says, and then,
after a pause, "I didn't want to miss you."

How she won't be denied, how
I resist. Ninety-two, she's the kind
of goodness brings trouble, the powerful
voice calling me in

evenings when I was a boy.
Maybe now it's her way
to know she is okay.
Yesterday she called four times

for help with the date, days of the week
refusing to stay in their places.
"It's Saturday," she says, a questioning in her voice, adding,
"I'm so confused, it's embarrassing."

I can see her calendar: she's crossed off Friday
and forgotten, now maybe Saturday, too.
"I'm sorry, I cause so much trouble," she says, starting to cry.
"It's okay, Ma, I mix up days, too.

Last week," I tell her,
"I drove to the wrong job."

Suddenly she laughs,
and I know it's okay, for the moment
neither hearing the powerful voice.

Resurrection

Michael Macklin

The night Bobby Inch died
my father came home wild-eyed and crying.
A cattle truck charging through the dusk
caught the paper boy high on its horns,
threw him breathless to one side.

We wore the same shirt that day.
In flashing reds and blues,
my father saw the shirt, still
against the blacktop.
Felt me slipping from him.

Seeing Bobby's face,
some other father's son,
he raced home to rage and rant
and hold me, looking deep
into my wide open eyes.

Hands Reaching

Edward J. Reilly

A young boy, I was primed
for climbing, eyeing the oats bin
and its top, a crosshatching of boards
flaked with end-of-year fragments
left over from the top's
double duty as a hayloft.

I climbed and climbed, up the wooden
ladder, foot reaching gingerly for
the next step, hands gripping and
pulling, even a young boy's weight heavy.
I made it and exulted, exulted

all too soon. There came a time
when getting down was even more vital
than climbing up. But that distance
multiplied looking down, and neither hands
nor feet could move me down that crawl.

So I called, and my brother answered,
years older, years taller, strong
shoulders and long arms stretching,
reaching my straining hands, my hands
in his, the rest of me coming naturally.

Years later my brother, in his quiet, dark
living room reached and fell,
his large, much older body tumbling
to the floor, silent on a carpet brown as hay,
leaving me nights I dream about long
arms reaching for a frightened boy.

Sentences

Edward Nobles

The sledgehammer cracks
like my father's heavy shouts
until the stone starts to break.
The sound then is different.
Only a thumb's touch is needed.
The division is final.

Where He Went

Edward Nobles

My father gave up
wife children friends
dog car house every
worldly possession
traveling
far into a strange
space bottles
rotating shuffling clinking
searching vaguely for a genie
poof!

Housekeeping of a Kind

Patricia Smith Ranzoni

Once in a great while this house reeks
with remembrances of Wild Rose rage.
The payday cheap gallon kind.
The silent supper kind.
The don't pay any attention to your father
when he is drinking kind.
The fist on the kitchen table pounding kind.
The maybe if I listen he'll like me kind.
The sinks into Kem-tone cover-ups
and scats along once-a-year-painted
battleship gray, worn to the black,
linoleum floor kind.
The wraps around frozen pipes and spills up
through cracked ceilings
and out leaking roofs kind.
The thirty years later
has to be reminded it was renovated out kind.

Stubborn stain.

The Crossing

David Walker

At the far edge of the field, just in the shade,
my father waves; the heat cuts us in two
as I walk towards him. The stubble bleeds
yellow, then nearly white; it crunches like snow.

Into the sun I stride, erect in my cause
and body straining towards the other side.
Hands on his hips, my father watches me cross
calmly. I am revolved in the season's eye.

The sun leans in the distance, drawing a cloak
of pines slowly over its head; and still
he is waiting. Every year that I walk
his smile grows nearer. And I begin to smile.

If You Should Die Before I Do

Patricia Smith Ranzoni

I'll come wherever you're praised.
Sit or stand in the back, *quietly,*

As I came whenever I came
among those you've loved. As any

grateful heart knows not how
to thank a source for song. At least

I knew you enough
to comprehend gave. If you should die first,

I'll come bare-footed when you
are alone. Don't worry, nothing tasteless

to clutter your grave,
only my dust and petals and pollens

from my beds to sift into yours,
and in this way I might come to hold you,

with the others,
perhaps forever.

Old

Philip Booth

Old, the old know cause to be bitter:
                                        they've seen
their children (as if they could tell)
insist they are growing deaf:
                                        they've found
old friends invent new friends
to prove the old don't matter:
                                        they have hardened
themselves to let memory rust out;
with only themselves to hold on to,
                                        they have grown
beyond any surprise;
to get their way
                                        they have aged again
to be children:
beyond control, they have gained
                                        control
of every last life save their own.
They know it can get no better.

The Cross of Snow

Henry Wadsworth Longfellow

In the long, sleepless watches of the night,
A gentle face — the face of one long dead —
Looks at me from the wall, where round its head
The night-lamp casts a halo of pure light.
Here in this room she died; and soul more white
Never through martyrdom of fire was led
To its repose; nor can in books be read
The legend of a life more benedight.

There is a mountain in the distant West
That, sun-defying, in its deep ravines
Displays a cross of snow upon its side.
Such is the cross I wear upon my breast
These eighteen years, through all the changing scenes
And seasons, changeless since the day she died.

The Power of It

Ted Bookey

Ruth woke sad today. Life, she says,
Has been behaving itself & hopeful
Expectations continue, so why now
Nameless dread & mope at sunrise?
What is it? What can it be?

I do not know but I will try.
To help her against it
— whatever it is
I put my arms around her,
Tell her, "What it is, is
There will come moments
When it is simply it."

I say this for myself
As much as for her —
That it is just it.

& it helps.

Sixty

Philip Booth

Spring hills, dark contraries:

a glade in a fall valley,
its one flower steeped with sun.

The there and here of her.
The soft where.

The sweet closeness of when.

From dreams awake to turn to her.
Remembering, remembering.

And now again. Again.

Feasting

Elizabeth W. Garber

I am so amazed to find myself kissing you
with such abandon,
filling myself with our kisses
astounding hunger for edges of lips and tongue.
                    Returning to feast again and again,
our bellies never overfilling from this banquet.
Returning in surprise,
in remembering,
in rediscovering,
such play of flavors of gliding lips
and forests of pressures and spaces.
The spaces between the branches
as delicious as finding the grove of lilies of the valley
blossoming just outside my door under the ancient oak.
"I've never held anyone this long," you said,
the second time you entered my kitchen.
I am the feast this kitchen was blessed to prepare
waiting for you to enter open mouthed in awe
in the mystery we've been given,
our holy feast.

Regeneration

Carolyn Locke

for Gerry

I heard how the starfish learns the world
through touch, how its chemical sense
leads it to the mussel bed, how it feels
its way around crevices sucking soft bodies
from their shells. You can't kill a starfish
in any usual way — chop one up
and it multiplies, filling the waters
with quintuples of spiny legs
reaching out from humped backs, and curling
around the deep purple shells on the rocky
bottom. Sometimes I think I know
what it is to know the world
through only the body. If I close my eyes,
I no longer feel where my body ends
and yours begins —
and I can believe your hands are mine
reaching for muscle,
a strange body becoming my own,
and in my ear an unfamiliar heartbeat
pumps new blood, breath no longer mine

doubles the lungs, my need
growing larger than what any body can hold
until there is only this way of knowing, this touch
that leads me, blind as the starfish,
to become what I cannot see.

2

The Place Inside the Place

The Glass Harmonica

Theodore Enslin

It snowed in far country
north and
beyond the trees.
As I went through the mirror
my breath froze
clouding it,
and they saw me no longer
in the villages of spring.
I walked alone
across level plains,
and my tracks disappeared
in the snow which went with me.
A wind rose
playing on harpstrings
and reeds.
There was nothing there, and my fingers
touched ice.
A music
a music
an echo of music —
sound not a sound
in the quiet north country —
the snow.

The Street

Lewis Turco

In the street the wind gutters, moving papers
and leaves into heaps or sworls.
The scraps of the year make some kind of pattern,
some calligramme of their own,
beyond the imprint of new snow.

Lightly, on the flourishes of silence,
on the heaps of leaf,
the snow touches and explores.
Finally, in folds of stillness,
flakes begin to form wrinkles of crystal.

By the time dusk deepens,
the wrinkles will be pure streams
drowning whatever is old.
Then, in the night, in the darkest hours,
the road will be a river of snow
aiming toward morning, lost at either end
in the curbs of vision.

Potatoes

Jay Davis

A family of potatoes lives under my sink.
They huddle there like wretched immigrants
in the hold of my kitchen, eyeing anyone
who peers down there with suspicion.
Despite the language barrier, they persist.
The more industrious put down roots.
They wear the same brown shabby coats
they brought from the old country,
though one or two are wrinkled now
from sleeping in them every night.
When the cupboard door is closed
I sense them in there, huddling closer,
muttering in their dark dialect, comforting
one another, whispering their dreams.

Winter Friends

Robert P. Tristram Coffin

The high cold moon rides through the frost,
The branches of the trees make lace
Along the drifted snow beneath,
There is no friendliness in the place,
Except in twelve small squares of light
Set in a house's midnight side.
Someone is awake with me
On the cold earth's wintry ride,
Through the pathways of the space,
He and I go on like friends,
Saying nothing, quietly,
To our separate unknown ends.

Essence

Stuart Kestenbaum

We hand-crank the drill through the maple's bark,
pound the metal tap into light inner layers

where the sap begins to flow, this life blood
that will make the leaves unfurl

in another two months, delicately
lined like the hands of a newborn.

But now we step over last year's leaves
and the year's before that

in patchy snow to gather what
we have taken from the tree, the gallons of sap

we boil down on our stove top,
moisture running off the kitchen windows

as we get down to its essence, over three gallons
to make a cup of syrup, so sweet

a transformation, I can't believe I could
have been a part of it. A world that doesn't

end in vinegar, ashes and regret,
but in a sweetness that rises every day

between earth and sky, traveling from the hole
in the side of the tree to our joyous mouths.

Porcupine

Tom Sexton

Its movement on
the ground is
that of a bag
of stones rolled
downhill, a spilled
quiver of blacktipped
arrows, but
now, on this
cold March morning,
it is raising the
dark flag of itself
to the top of
an ancient tree
like an explorer
claiming the world
in the name
of all that is Porcupine.

Mud Season

Alice Persons

After a brutal Maine winter
the world dissolves
in weak sunshine and water:
Mud sucks at your shoes.
It's impossible to keep the floors
or the dogs clean.
Peeling layers of clothes, you emerge
pale, root-like, a little dazed
by brighter light.
You haven't looked at your legs
in months
and discover an alarming new geography
of veins and flaws.
Last year you scoffed at people
who got spray-tanned
but it's starting to appeal.
Your only consolation is the company of others
who haven't been to Nevis
or Boca Raton,
a pale army
of fellow radishes,
round onions,
long-underground tubers.

Night Wind in Spring

Elizabeth Coatsworth

Two yellow dandelion shields do not make spring,
nor do the wild duck swimming by the shore,
so self-possessed, so white of side and breast,
nor, I suppose, the change in the land-birds' calls,
softened and sweetened to a courting note,
nor the new colors twigs are taking on,
not even the sun which rises early now
and lingers almost until dinner time.
We, too, are valid instruments; we, too, can say
if this be spring or only waning winter.
Tonight the wind is loud about our chimney.
There is no new moon in the sky, nothing but stars:
the Dipper upright on its shining handle,
Sirius bright above a neighbor's house,
and this wind roaming, not enough to scrape
a branch along the roof, or try the shutters
for one to bang. No, just enough to cry
and cry and cry against the stalwart chimney,
as though it were a wanderer who had come
down half the world to find one only door
and that door locked and nothing answering.

April and Then May

Kate Barnes

April and then May,
violets up in the field,
the ewes with their twin lambs;

time has decided
to turn into spring again
after all.

The maples are unfolding their leaves,
chives stand green at the kitchen door,
the black flies have decided to come back;

and the work mare has her new foal
capering over bluets in the pasture,
and the hall smells of daffodils;

and everything
is divinely ordinary —
the deep ruts in the field track,

the spring overflowing,
the excited swallows,
the apple trees

budding for perhaps the hundredth time —
and the pruned boughs budding too
that must bloom just where they lie.

Stealing Lilacs

Alice Persons

A guaranteed miracle,
it happens for two weeks each May,
this bounty of riches
where McMansion, trailer,
the humblest driveway
burst with color — pale lavender,
purple, darker plum —
and glorious scent.
This morning a battered station wagon
drew up on my street
and a very fat woman got out
and starting tearing branches
from my neighbor's tall old lilac —
grabbing, snapping stems, heaving
armloads of purple sprays
into her beater.
A tangle of kids' arms and legs
writhed in the car.
I almost opened the screen door
to say something,
but couldn't begrudge her theft,
or the impulse
to steal such beauty.
Just this once,
there is enough for everyone.

The Poet

Marta Rijn Finch

Heard you were moving in last week. Welcome.
You'll like it here. The people — most of them —
are friendly. You'll meet them tomorrow at church.
There's a bean supper afterward. Real nice folks.
Hard-working. But an old crone lives down
the street with a couple cats — three, maybe four.
Keeps to herself so we hardly know she's there.
She's got a daughter no one's ever seen;
visits her son somewhere over the border.
She has no flag, but hangs the hammock out;
that tells us she's in residence. We see it
from the shore — and smoke, of course, come winter.
They say she is a poet. I don't know.
I've never seen it. Can't be any good.
She read her poems once at the library,
but no one went. Not even the local teacher.
Just the librarian. She *had* to be there.
And a lot of folks drove up from away.

You don't write poetry, do you?

How to Catch a Poem

Robert Siegel

It begins with one leaf rubbing against another,
a light, a rift in a cloud, the weight of a feather
spiraling down, a ripple on the water —

its shape rising from the dark and fusing
with a sound, a touch, a peculiar scent. Now it begins
to show plumage, the gleam of a pelt, pausing

to stare with an ebony eye. One twitch — it's gone,
fled into that darker wood behind the eyes. Stunned,
you trace its tracks on paper, stumble,

pick yourself up and go down each sly
cheat of a path vanishing in a thicket, lie
still, listening for its breath, a twig breaking

where you think. . . . Avoid sleep, follow all day,
at night listen for its cry under the moon. Finally you may
gather enough to show its presence. Delay

finishing what you have. Take your time. Return home
and frame the cast of its footprint: that is the poem.

In Nightgowns

Sheila Gray Jordan

Nothing insists they get dressed.
Midmorning, like toddlers,
late parading in their pajamas,
they walk out of the house
in nightgowns.

What do they care who sees them
without a robe, appearing
in the first layer over
the Emperor's new clothes,
these elderly women

sweeping the steps, accommodating
an arthritic cocker spaniel,
dead-heading the lilies.
Or they proceed like butterflies,
pastel-bright, to flutter

from this to that, breezy —
not explaining —
in and out of sun and shade,
air reaching up under
a skirt.

Night

Louise Bogan

The cold remote islands
And the blue estuaries
Where what breathes, breathes
The restless wind of the inlets,
And what drinks, drinks
The incoming tide;

Where shell and weed
Wait upon the salt wash of the sea,
And the clear nights of stars
Swing their lights westward
To set behind the land;

Where the pulse clinging to the rocks
Renews itself forever;
Where, again on cloudless nights,
The water reflects
The firmament's partial setting;

— O remember
In your narrowing dark hours
That more things move
Than blood in the heart.

Some Clear Night

Gary Lawless

Some clear night like this,
when the stars are all out and shining,
our old dogs will come back to us,
out of the woods, and lead us
along the stone wall to the cove.
There will be foxes, and loons,
and a houseboat floating on the lake.
The trees will lean in, a lantern
swinging over the water, the creaking of oars.
Now we will learn the true names of the stars.
Now we will know what the trees are saying.
There is wood in the stove.
We left the front door open.
Does the farmhouse know
that we're never coming back?

Which World

Gary Lawless

There is a path
winding between Sitka spruce,
past totem poles stolen
from their island homes,
emptied of ashes and bones,
placed along the trail.
In the distance,
a volcano.
Raven flies
just above the surface of things, bald
eagle watching through
layers of air and water
for the fish
passing through,
shining in the cold
river like light
from another world,
everything moving, everything
moving to
come together, come together and
fall apart, again.
the water rushing.
the heart beating.
I am waiting for you
at the mouth of the river.

Driving Down East

Robert M. Chute

Crossing the Penobscot on Route One
we enter a different country. Our home state
on both sides of course, all part of the Main,
but the dull green rainbow bridge was a
suspension of disbelief as well as steel.

At Verona Island we expected a guard house
with a deadpan downeaster in oilskins to
silently check our visas and wave us through.

The houses were familiar clapboard and shingle
but smaller, pinched between wild lands,
barrens and ledges edging the sea. Life
on our inland lakes with its jumble of cobbles
seemed safe but not these wave-scoured ledges.

Life on the edge salts speech with words
as strange to us as to Summer People. Words
regional, individual, or invented to toll the tourists.

Everyone is "from away": we are, they are,
but all in one bag together in the final drag
dumped on the deck for culling.

The Red and Green Cement Truck

Richard Aldridge

rumbles by to where it's going, while
at an incline on the bed and
at right angles to the wheels
its mixer, shaped
like a big cocktail shaker, turns
upon an axis slowly, slowly,
blending the cement and water.

It is a feat as neat as
pat-your-head-and-rub-your-belly
but what I like still better is
to see in it
ourselves, we who do best
to use our heads for mulling, mixing
while with our feet
we keep on trucking.

The Dump Pickers

Bruce Guernsey

On Sundays
carting my trash to the dump
I'd see them swarming
the piles like gnats,
a whole family of pickers
straight from Mass:
Dad's suit, white
as the noon sky, Junior
in a polka-dot tie —
in bright, patent leathers
his small, pale sister.

From the highest of piles
Mother shouted orders
through a paper cup,
the men hurrying under
her red, high heels,
dragging metal to the pickup,
the little girl giggling,
spinning on her toes
through the blowing paper
like a dancer, a little twist
of wind in the dust.

Understory

Jim Glenn Thatcher

The old man had always been a mystery,
living out there on that abandoned logging road
in those miles of woods between the Parsonsfields.
Months would go by without anyone seeing him.
No one even noticed when he first went missing.
Gone for all of seven seasons before a hunter found him —
not in those open pine woods where they'd sometimes
seen him ranging, but tangled beneath the understory
less than a hundred yards behind his shack.
Stripped down to rags on a skeleton, bedded
in spears of burdock; ribs twined with creeper;
his skull filled now with the strangeness of other life,
the sun tracking its daily course of shadow and light
along the brow of the caves where his eyes had been.

When they went in to clean out his shack,
not expecting much — a rotting cot,
a very old sleeping bag, some utensils, one cup.
It was the notebooks that surprised them.
Piles upon piles of old notebooks, all of them full —
"Crawling with words," someone said. A library of wildness —
journal entries that seem written by the forest itself,
the woods he lived in become the woods living in him.
Passages of a feral intelligence hedging off into its hinterlands —
stories of stones, autobiographies of oaks and maples,

a runic hand-scrawl scratching itself into granite,
sand, leaf, bough, fin, fur, feather, claw,
the commonality of bark and blood and bone —
histories of a self gone Other. . .

Mantis

Robert Siegel

Still as a silk screen I wait, I wait,
invisible, part of the furniture,
for the ambling fly or worm,
the Monarch just alighting,
the beetle dark under its armor.
On the altar of my arms, I offer up
whatever wanders by. In love
I am insatiable, will take
my mate's head in his electric need
and devour it, swallowing his body
almost as an afterthought;
then, absent-mindedly,
moving stiff and brittle as a tree,
go propagate my kind.

Moth at My Window

Richard Aldridge

Against my pane
He beats a rapid
Pitapat
In trying to reach
The desk lamp lit
In front of me.
Wing flurries spent,
He crawls and toils
This way and that,
His whole self bound
To pierce the veil
He cannot see.

The glance I turn
On him, light
Spreading still across
My page, is one
Of interest in
The company.
Whatever time
I take to watch
Will be no loss
From my own toils
To pierce the veil
I cannot see.

Garden Spider

Richard Foerster

Argiope bruennichi

An orbweaver, adrift among
the hosta's spent stalks, black
and brilliant-banded gold, dead-

center in a mist of silks and two
zigzag vertical rays strung as luminous
warning to any flying bird, hovered

last evening, head earthward, her legs
poised to set the web trembling to a blur
each time I crouched to watch, spell-

bound and snared with the thought
that here's the perfect fretwork
to grace a backyard garden. Now

this morning I see she's consumed
each filament, digested the indispensible
proteins to respin the entire design

somewhere away from my quisitive gaze.
What must I admire, left with empty
space: an unbending mind

fixed on private workings, or the way
the very fabric of a world
can be chewed up for weaving again?

Lost Graveyards

Elizabeth Coatsworth

In Maine the dead
melt into the forest
like Indians, or, rather,
in Maine the forests shadow round the dead
until the dead are indistinguishably mingled
with trees; while underground,
roots and bones intertwine,
and above earth
the tilted gravestones, lichen-covered, too,
shine faintly out from among pines and birches,
burial stones and trunks
growing together
above the lattices of roots and bones.
Now is the battle over,
the harsh struggle
between man and the forest.
While they lived,
these men and women fought the encroaching trees,
hacked them with axes,
severed them with saws,
burned them in fires,
pushed them back and back
to their last lairs among the shaggy hills,
while the green fields lay tame about the houses.
Living they fought the wild,

but dead, they rested,
and the wild softly, silently, secretly,
returned. In Maine
the dead sooner or later feel the hug of rootlets,
and shadowy branches closing out the sun.

Gulls in Wind

Betsy Sholl

Bedraggled feathers like bonnets
that would fly off if they weren't strapped,
kazoo-voiced, a chorus of crying dolphins
or rusty sirens a speck of dust could set off —
these raucous gleaners milling around

pick up and discard, now a Q-tip,
now a shred of lettuce or cellophane,
a cigarette butt one holds a second
as if he really might smoke. One drags
an old condom, one spots a good crumb

and walk-runs, squawks everyone else away.
But it's just a dried scrap of weed he'll toss back,
grist for the next fool's expectation.
Still, a loud alpha catches wind,
scoots over to check it out. Shove off,

he screeches, this is my no-good, barren,
motel-infested spit of sand — on which
he neither toils nor spins, but grubs all day
on webbed feet and clever back-hinged knees,
now skittishly sidestepping a gusty

piece of plastic blown against his legs,
hopping to get it off, now shaking it
once or twice to make sure it's worthless
before he turns his face to the wind,
letting it smooth his fine fractious feathers.

The Habitation

Lewis Turco

There is no way out.
Now the windows have begun
to cloud over: cobwebs, dust.
The stairs and floors are unstable —
the hours nibble the foundations.

In the bedrooms, sheets
have begun to yellow, spreads
to fray. Coverlets have worn
to the colors of late autumn,
thin as a draft sifting at the sill.

On the kitchen floor
crumbs and rinds lie recalling
the old feasts. In the larder
preserves rust among speckled jars;
the bins yawn; shadow sates the cupboards.

The fire has been damped
at the hearth: its bed of ash
sinks in pit-holes over brick.
The ceiling snows on the carpet —
Rejoice! Rejoice! The house is failing!

The Last Lamp-Lighters

Kenneth Rosen

I saw the last lamp-lighters! Patrolling
        The dusk, looking for gas-lamps
Whose lights had gone out. Each held a pole
Forked for lifting the frail pearl-tinted bowl,
And one with a small wheel and flint for casting

A spark. Did all lamps need to be lit? Or just
        Those doused by raindrops or errant drafts?
They seemed sad, these doomed men who knew
How to give fog its soft perfume, and the facts
Of our life their necessary, tender, but fatal glow.

Closing Time

Dave Morrison

The bartender has just announced last call.
It feels like bedtime did when we were young;
we act surprised, and then we act appalled.
It's much too soon, and we aren't nearly done,
but just like then, no matter what we say,
we have to move along, we cannot stay.

The bouncer has a sideshow barker's call:
"Come on people, drink 'em up, let's go,
it's hotel-motel time, the clock on the wall
says that this bar ain't open any more. . ."
When lights come on it's unnerving to see
the club in all its tattered misery.

The soundman coils the cables on the stage
just like a sailor making fast his ship.
The weary waitress starts to feel her age
and rubs her temples while she counts her tips.
The barback lugs the cases up the stairs
and fills the coolers with tomorrow's beers.

The sadness of anonymous goodbyes —
we drain our drinks and shuffle out the door
to make our way back to whatever lives
we left to come here several hours before.
Unfinished business always seems to shape
our attempts at transformation and escape.

3

Changes of Heart

The Net

Peter Harris

I saw the black maid park the Cadillac
in the lot of the Indian Harbor Yacht Club.
When she hefted the first huge silver tray
of delicacies for that evening's soiree
on her boss' yacht, I offered to help.

No, she said, in her starched gray uniform
on orders from her employer. The launch man
in wrinkled khakis and a black cap with gold
braided on the bill, told her no, she couldn't
ride the launch. Against Club rules.

But I am just bringing out the food, she said.
Everyone looked at the ground. The launch man
and the maid in their uniforms with strict orders,
me, at twelve, with my marlin spike and stopwatch,
still learning the lines, the tactics of yachting.

I'd never been so close to a black person.
I could see the whites of her eyes flash.
She was caught. He was caught. I
didn't know that I'd been caught. I couldn't
feel the hook that pinned my tongue to my cheek.

But stepping aboard the launch, I felt the net,
woven so carefully by so many hands,
the seamless, almost miraculously strong,
transparent canopy that would keep everyone
in Greenwich exquisitely and forever in place.

Making the Turn

Sarah Jane Woolf-Wade

There comes a time
with dependable rhythm
every year
late in August
when the wind turns around,
blows in air from the north
to chill the bay
and the year turns its face
away from summer.

Monarch butterflies
ripple down to zinnias that bend
toward late afternoon sun,
bank their wings
and lean into the last leg
of their unavoidable flight plan.

Sometime in every life
there comes that inevitable turn
when we face away. . .
I can't be sure when that moment was for me.

The Geese

May Sarton

The geese honked overhead.
I ran to catch the skein
To watch them as they fled
In a long wavering line.

I caught my breath, alone,
Abandoned like a lover
With winter at the bone
To see the geese go over.

It happens every year
And every year some woman
Haunted by loss and fear
Must take it as an omen,

Must shiver as she stands
Watching the wild geese go,
With sudden empty hands
Before the cruel snow.

Some woman every year
Must catch her breath and weep
With so much wildness near
At all she cannot keep.

Inland

Edna St. Vincent Millay

People that build their houses inland,
    People that buy a plot of ground
Shaped like a house, and build a house there,
    Far from the sea-board, far from the sound

Of water sucking the hollow ledges,
    Tons of water striking the shore, —
What do they long for, as I long for
    One salt smell of the sea once more?

People the waves have not awakened,
    Spanking the boats at the harbour's head,
What do they long for, as I long for, —
    Starting up in my inland bed,

Beating the narrow walls, and finding
    Neither a window nor a door,
Screaming to God for death by drowning, —
    One salt taste of the sea once more?

Hearing Your Words, and Not a Word Among Them

Edna St. Vincent Millay

Hearing your words, and not a word among them
Tuned to my liking, on a salty day
When inland woods were pushed by winds that flung them
Hissing to leeward like a ton of spray;
I thought how off Matinicus the tide
Came pounding in, came running though the Gut,
While from the Rock the morning whistle cried,
And children whimpered and the doors blew shut;
There in the autumn when the men go forth,
In gardens stripped and scattered, peering north,
With dahlia tubers dripping from the hand:
The wind of their endurance, driving south,
Flattened your words against your speaking mouth.

Humane Society

Bruce Spang

The neighbor's pup,
wanting in,
won't let up.
Yelp. Yelp. Yelp.
This, the fourth night
of its desperation.

Our two cats huddle
at the open window
pretending to be sympathetic.
Downstairs, the cuckoo pleads
its shrill three-stress call.

I can remember,
shivering in my pajamas,
calling out, again and again,
Sandy, Sandy, Sandy,
drifting into blackness.
Leave it alone, My wife would intone.
Let it learn.

But it was not the dog I was calling,
not then, when my marriage
could be counted in the three-word
sentences we barked between us.

It was my wanting out, there
on the porch in the cold,
waiting to hear how far my voice
could carry across night fields.

Reuben Bright

Edwin Arlington Robinson

Because he was a butcher and thereby
Did earn an honest living (and did right),
I would not have you think that Reuben Bright
Was any more a brute than you or I;
For when they told him that his wife must die,
He stared at them, and shook with grief and fright,
And cried like a great baby half that night,
And made the women cry to see him cry.

And after she was dead, and he had paid
The singers and the sexton and the rest,
He packed a lot of things that she had made
Most mournfully away in an old chest
Of hers, and put some chopped-up cedar boughs
In with them, and tore down the slaughter house.

Sudden Death

Linda Buckmaster

You were an electric current leaping
between contact points, living always
so bright, so hot until
that moment

you shorted out, caught fire, and
bursting into white flames,
consumed yourself
in light and heat, leaving us
the still warm ashes of an afterlife.

January

Linda Buckmaster

The other night, I saw you
as moonlight coming in
the west window of the kitchen.
Fourteen years in this house and I never
before saw the moon coming in that particular window.
Perhaps it's that we never stayed up so late,
at least not on bright nights in winter when
the low-slung moon moves around
the corner of the house and into the side yard. Or
perhaps it's just that I never noticed before now. Now

I'm often up very late, alone,
so that night I saw you softly spreading
across the dark countertop and burnished surface
of the stove — a triangle of light — and
I lowered my face and kissed you.

A Little Bit of Timely Advice

Mekeel McBride

Time you put on blue
shoes, high-heeled, sequined,
took yourself out dancing.

You been spending too much
time crying salty
dead-fish lakes into soupspoons,

holding look-alike contests
with doom. Baby, you
need to be moving. Ruin

ruins itself, no use unplanting
what's left of your garden.
Crank up the old radio

into lion-looking-for-food
music; or harmonica, all indigo,
breathing up sunrise. Down

and out's just another opinion
on up and over. You say
you got no makings

for a song? Sing anyway.
Best music's the stuff comes
rising out of nothing.

Early Morning Trumpet

George V. Van Deventer

for Gabe

On occasion, leaving the barn
after milking, I'd hear
my neighbor's son down the valley,
across the stream, play
his trumpet as if he were thinking out loud, moving
in the privacy of his thoughts.
I'd stop as if it were a call to prayer
and follow his flight,
as I would follow a nuthatch
piping from tree to tree —
a personal song
unfolding around me.

April Prayer

Stuart Kestenbaum

Just before the green begins there is the hint of green
a blush of color, and the red buds thicken
the ends of the maple's branches and everything
is poised before the start of a new world,
which is really the same world
just moving forward from bud
to flower to blossom to fruit
to harvest to sweet sleep, and the roots
await the next signal, every signal
every call a miracle and the switchboard
is lighting up and the operators are
standing by in the pledge drive we've
all been listening to: Go make the call.

Transportation

Kristen Lindquist

Everyone in O'Hare is happy today.
Sun shines benevolently
onto glorious packaged snack foods
and racks of Bulls T-shirts.
My plane was twenty minutes early.
Even before I descend into the trippy light show
of the walkway between terminals,
I am ecstatic. I can't stop smiling.
On my flight we saw Niagara Falls
and Middle America green and gold below.
Passengers thanked the pilot for his smooth landing
with such gratitude that I too
thanked him, with sudden and wholehearted sincerity.
A group of schoolchildren passes on the escalator,
and I want to ask where they're going.
Tell me your story, I want to say.
This is life in motion.
A young couple embraces tearfully at a gate;
she's leaving, he's not.
How can I bring this new self back to you, intact?
He yells to her departing back,
"Hey, I like the way you move!"
Any kind of love seems possible.
We walk through this light together.
So what if it's an airport?
So what if it won't last?

Nude

Robert Siegel

Content in her skin she does not challenge
the blue shadow cast over much of her body,
waiting in the shade like a center of gravity,
so full, even the trees have travelled too far.

Her breasts steal the wind with surprise,
promise long savannahs of discovery
beyond the trembling compass of a flower
or tuft of weeds agog with her sweet breath.

I stand in this museum looking,
blood sagging to my fingers and toes.
The sun is coming at me through the wall.
Clothes could never touch her, this one, put
beyond the night whisper and morning's flat red mouth
into the first turning of the light.

The Alligator's Hum

Kenneth Rosen

To allure an alligator lady so she'll allow him
To fertilize her eggs before she buries them
In her sand nest, the male alligator
Hums in a swamp pond like a kid in a bathtub.
It hums like a foghorn: *Hummmmmm!* And raises
Queer geysers of water by his torso's profound
Vibrations, these inverted, fragile, almost crystal
Chandeliers his obligatto of amor. I have tried this
On dates without knowing what I was doing:
Hummmmmm! My date pretended she didn't know
What I was doing either and would ask,
"Are you all right?" *Hmmmmmm!* I'd echo,

Something below my solar plexus now governing
My lowest, reptilian, ganglion brain. But I swear,
Like people who claim they can't understand poetry,
She knew what it meant for the hum of the body
To dominate mind. It meant please admire
My wet inverted chandeliers, which translates
Like all poetry too, into alligator: "You can get me,
If you let me, you grinning, beautiful
primordial swampwater creature you!" Then their tails
Slap the water with a belly whomp.
They thrash like mad, almost invincible — though the human
Eye is never naked — and then it's over.

Ball Smacks Mouth, Splits Lip

Bob MacLaughlin

Marietta Mansfield came walking up
the driveway while I was playing catch
with her brother on the grass,
so I, who had it bad for Marietta Mansfield,
looked over at her an instant before the ball
smacked me in the mouth, splitting my upper lip.

Their mother took me to Dr. Waddle, who stitched
the pieces back together well enough
for Marietta Mansfield to kiss me on that mouth
a month later in a dark ping-pong room.

The next morning I went away to summer camp,
where I played on the baseball team
and wrote letters to Marietta Mansfield
every day, and she to me, until hers stopped,
whereupon I fell into a terrible batting slump.

After camp I went off to high school in the next town,
but Marietta Mansfield was still in eighth grade
so I hardly ever saw her, ignored her when I did,
said snide things she could overhear
so she would feel as bad as I felt.

Years later, when I found out our letters
had been shortstopped by her mother,
I felt even worse.

Sandwiches

Pam Burr Smith

When I was young
My mother made me sandwiches for lunch
Butter on one slice of bread
Mayo on the other
Lettuce and tomato
Bologna or salami
Two slices always
Or tuna salad or meatloaf

These were big thick sandwiches
That could fall apart

Not like those one slice of bread
One slice of ham
One slice of bread sandwiches
The cool kids had

I wanted everything the cool kids had
And I wanted their dry little sandwiches, too

Mine were so obviously made by a mother
Clumsy in their over-love
Every taste and vitamin she could pack into them
Every morning too full too full
I needed two napkins to eat them

Not like the cool kids
Who could hold a neat little sandwich
In one hand
While mine dribbled love
Down my arm

The Goldfish

Mekeel McBride

It was a feeder, which means it was supposed
to get fed to something bigger like a barracuda.
But I put the ten-cent comet in clean water
with enough food, no predators, and it grew
into a radiant glider full of happy appetite.

That was the truth of it for a long time and then
the fish, for no reason that I could see, suddenly
curled upside down into a red question mark.
Now, its golden scales drop off like sequins
from a museum dress and its mouth forms over

and over the same empty O. Though I wish to,
there's no way to free it, not even for a second,
from its own slow death. You say this fish is the least
of it, that I'd better start worrying about what's
really wrong: a child chained somewhere

in a basement, starving; the droop-eyed man,
cooking up, in a cast-iron kettle, germ stew
that will end the world. But that's exactly what I said.
The golden thing is dying right on the other side
of the glass; I can see it and there's nothing I can do.

The Plymouth on Ice

Thomas R. Moore

On frigid January nights we'd
take my 'forty-eight Plymouth onto
the local reservoir, lights off
to dodge the cops, take turns

holding long manila lines in pairs
behind the car, cutting colossal
loops and swoons across
the crackly range of ice. Oh

God, did we have fun! At ridges
and fissures we careened,
tumbled onto each other, the girls
yelping, splayed out on all fours,

and sometimes we heard groans
deep along the fracture lines as
we spun off in twos, to paw, clumsy,
under parkas, never thinking of

love's falls or how thin ice
would ease us into certain death.
No, death was never on our minds,
we were eighteen, caterwauling

under our own moon that
warded off cops and
front-page stories of six kids
slipping under the fickle surface.

The Hands

Bruce Guernsey

The only time we touch now
is in our sleep, as if our hands,
finding each other,
have lives of their own.

Joined to our surprise every morning,
they are full of longing,
like a one-armed man
trying to pray.

We pull them apart
starting the day, yours
to your work, mine to mine:
purses, pockets, change.

How they love the night,
the cool of linen, the underside
of pillows — sneaking out,
meeting without us in the dark.

Theirs is a language we've forgotten,
a way of speaking now their own:
touching, whispering,
making plans.

Divorce

Donald Crane

She got the path to the spring house
through the asters and fireweed
and the orange "touch me not."

The gray smudges that are deer
at the far edge of the pasture at dusk.

The broad leaves of the rhubarb plant
where early in the morning
the swallowtail butterflies lie
motionless with their wings spread
to dry.

Redtail hawks overhead; jays fussing
in the apple orchard gone wild.

And from the kitchen window; the faint
haze in September over Tunk Mountain
20 miles away.

I got pigeons and starlings in the Bangor
city park, and a job stacking boxes
at the Mall.

Feed My Birds

Elizabeth McFarland

Feed my birds,
But not the whitethroat in his cage of air!
Feed robin, hawk,
The attendant flock
Of rooftree birds, and birds of prey or prayer;
But not the lost love calling, calling there.

At that wild voice
Trees touch their tips together and rejoice,
Rising full-leaved through waterfalls of sound.
That evergreen lament
Beyond all words has sent
Touch as soft as moss on woodland limbs unbound.

O feed them, scatter seed upon the ground!
Feed homing dove and jay,
Chickadees in black beret,
Feed simple starling, thrush, and small-shawled wren;
But sparrow, the white-throated one,
Feed not again!

Hummingbird

Ellen M. Taylor

A hummingbird's heart
beats 250 times per minute
when resting
and 1200 times while feeding.
A surprise can trigger
cardiac arrest,
as his tiny heart
cannot withstand
further stress.

I mourn
the ruby-throated juvenile
anxiously feeding in the phlox
this still September morning.
His whirring startled me
while I knelt to deadhead pansies —
I swatted at the sound,
and he fell.

Hen

Ellen M. Taylor

How does she do it, create such perfect
spheres within her feathered body? Every
twenty-four hours she leaves us, still warm,
an umber shell, inside it a yolk, ochre
and richer than butter, nested in white clear
as rainwater. She coos and clucks with content.

Loon Return

Carol Willette Bachofner

Long ribbons of loons
descend through a cleft
in the spreading morning;
resplendent in formal attire,
they dip into icy meltwater ponds.
Beautiful, eerie laughter heralds
oncoming spring, breaks the boreal
winter silence with its return.

Regret

Bob Brooks

It's like skipping a stone —
one thing reminds me of another.
And when the stone sinks,
I don't go after it.

I don't go after it.
But when the stone sinks,
it reminds me of another.

Another regret
like a skipping stone
I don't go after —

another stone,
sinking.

Snap

Bob Brooks

Poor mousie
living for months

on toilet paper
from the linen closet

one day finds bagels
and English muffins
in a kitchen cupboard

thinks she's died
and gone to heaven

yep

He Sees the Future

Dave Morrison

Her fingers flutter light, like butterflies.
The bass notes belt him like a boxer's gloves —
amazing octave leaps for such small hands.
She's pretty, sure, and young but that's not why
he stands and stares and falls mutely in love.

Her body and the bass's form a curve
that follows from her right hand to her left.
She looks as if she's watching weather come
or trying to place a stranger in a crowd.
She lets herself become lost in the sound,
and now she's trying to find her way back home.

She doesn't seem concerned about the band
or audience; she plays for someone else
he remembers when his playing caused a stir.
Now that seems a long, long time ago.
He feels like a distracted dinosaur
watching the approaching meteor.

Musician

Louise Bogan

Where have these hands been,
By what delayed,
That so long stayed
Apart from the thin

Strings which they now grace
With their lonely skill?
Music and their cool will
At last interlace.

Now with great ease, and slow,
The thumb, the finger, the strong
Delicate hand plucks the long
String it was born to know.

And, under the palm, the string
Sings as it wished to sing.

Today, the Traffic Signals All Changed for Me

Martin Steingesser

It's all language, I am thinking
on my way over the drawbridge to South Portland,
driving into a wishbone blue, autumn sky, maple
red, aspen yellow — oaks, evergreens
stretching out in sunlight. Isn't this all
message and sign, singing to us?
When I open ears, listen with eyes
wide open, the world tumbles in, suddenly
a rush through my body, how tires zummmmm
across a bridge grating, sending vibratos
along limbs, out fingers
and toes. Even these dead things
we make: cement walkways,
macadam streets, all our brick and steel
and rubber, even these are alive. Sometimes
I feel so empty. Today, I am filling up, the way
this Indian Summer morning keeps fattening
on sunlight, feelings, words frothing like yeast.
Blue sky rises in my blood, geese
and monarchs migrating through; my love's an open field,
meadows of goldfinch, Anne's lace, new moon
and crow laughing. . . Tornadoes
collapse in a breath, oceans curl at my toes, galaxies
exploding in my heart. Am I going loco? I pull over

onto the roadside, cars and trucks whizzing by.
I can't get places I thought I was going. I think of old Walt,
quadrupeds and birds stucco'd all over. Why not?
And you, too, Allen, gay, locomotive sunflower laureate,
both of you, among the leaves, in your all-star colors,
hitting all the curves, belting poems
out of the century. O look! — this is what's happening.

Last Writes

Carl Little

I tinker with most of my poems even after publication. I expect to be revising in my coffin as it is being lowered into the ground.
— Charles Simic

At the wake for the ex-U.S. poet laureate
at the Hotel Fin du Monde someone swore
he heard a scratching sound in the casket

and later, as we wedged the box into
a rocky corner of a New Hampshire bone orchard,
one of the pall bearers, a pallid poet with

acute hearing, caught the sibilant sound
of the words being crossed out — "kissing"
substituted for "praying," perhaps, or

"lover" for "beloved" — the gentle rub
of eraser, the whisper of a breath
to remove residue from the paper

and the click of the miner's lamp
Simic insisted wearing on his head
in lieu of the standard issue laurel wreath.

4

The World and Back Again

What Positions Do They and We Assume in the Encapsulated Stillness?

John Tagliabue

While
somewhere in a capsule deep in the sea
          off the Florida coast
seven visitors to the earth who planned to
          visit outer space
lie dead with their advanced technological gadgets
          and once active
mysterious eyes, all kinds of scientists and many
          argumentative committees
discuss in details the possible causes of the Challenger's
          explosion, flaming
demise into fish-wandering seas. Octopus nearby,
          and dead sea captains,
ships like old cultures gone to the bottom. The many
          slightly alive
statisticians argue and probe and computers they think
          are at their advanced
command. How silent they are, the sky dreamers, those
          children in the womb
          of the metal.

For the Falling Man

Annie Farnsworth

I see you again and again
tumbling out of the sky,
in your slate-gray suit and pressed white shirt.
At first I thought you were debris
from the explosion, maybe gray plaster wall
or fuselage but then I realized
that people were leaping.
I know who you are, I know
there's more to you than just this image
on the news, this ragdoll plummeting —
I know you were someone's lover, husband,
daddy. Last night you read stories
to your children, tucked them in, then curled into sleep
next to your wife. Perhaps there was small
sleepy talk of the future. Then,
before your morning coffee had cooled
you'd come to this; a choice between fire
or falling.
How feeble these words, billowing
in this aftermath, how ineffectual
this utterance of sorrow. We can see plainly
it's hopeless, even as the words trail from our mouths
— but we can't help ourselves — how I wish
we could trade them for something
that could really have caught you.

United States

Philip Booth

All right, we are two nations.

Immaculate floors, ceilings broken
only by skylights. The insulated
walls, the soundless heat; and hidden
everywhere, a fan for every odor.

Of our two nations
that is one.
                    And you who will not
read this
              presume you know the other.

Airfield

Robert Siegel

All day the great planes gingerly descend
an invisible staircase, holding up
their skirts and dignity like great ladies
in technicolor histories, or reascend,
their noses needling upward like a compass
into a wild blue vacuum,
leaving everything in confusion behind:

In some such self-deceiving light as this
we'll view the air force base when moved away
from where its sleepless eye revolves all night.
We'll smile and recollect it conversationally —
tell with what ease the silver planes dropped down
or how they, weightless, rose above
our roof. We'll pass it with a sugar and cream,

forever sheltered from this moment's sick
surprise that we have lived with terror, with pride,
the wounded god circling the globe, never resting,
that in the morning and the evening we have heard
his cry, have seen him drag his silver wings
whining with anguish like a huge
fly seeking to lay its deadly eggs.

Night Patrol

Bruce Guernsey

My father never slept real well after the war
and as my mother tells, he woke in fear
so deep, so far away, he seemed to stare
straight out at nothing she could see or hear.

Or worse — she wraps her robe around her, remembering —
he'd sit there grinning, bolt upright beside her,
this mad look on his face, the bed springs quivering
with some hilarity the night had whispered.

And once, "He did this, your father, I swear he did —
he must have been still dreaming, rest his soul —
he tried to close my frightened eyes, my lids,
to thumb them shut like he was on patrol

the way he'd learned so they would sleep, the dead.
And then he blessed himself and bowed his head."

Unknown Algonquin Females, Circa 1800s

Carol Willette Bachofner

They dug up my grandmother, moved her
to the museum. No one stopped them.
I had no say. De-recognized by government,
filed at the BIA under "I" (*Indian, former*),
she's been reduced to anthropology, curated
by bureaucrats, her bones on display
with the bones of a woman from an enemy tribe:
(*Unknown Algonquin Females, Circa 1800s*)
No one sang a travel song for her to ease her bones
along the way; no giveaway, no mourning strings
to soften the sorrow. I have watched their grandmas
prayed and cried into the ground, names cut
into marble, bodies preserved under stones safe
behind iron gates. The governor's announcement claims
today: *There are no Abenaki Indians left in Vermont.*

Nobody at Treblinka

Thomas Carper

Sie waren nicht ein kleiner Mann.
— Film director Claude Lanzmann
to a former Nazi official

But keep the scale in mind. What single man
Could undertake that kind of enterprise
When each day trains from half of Europe ran
Into the camp? The prisoners swarmed like flies
Onto the platforms. Hundreds did their jobs
Of keeping books, processing and selecting,
Or guarding work brigades, or moving mobs
Into the chambers . . . cleaning . . . disinfecting.
You see, with those large numbers, no one said,
"X is responsible." We were a team
Handling the hordes — the living, and the dead.
Mine was a minor function. Do I seem
Like someone who would cause such sufferings?
I was a nobody. Nobody does those things.

To Jesus on His Birthday

Edna St. Vincent Millay

For this your mother sweated in the cold,
For this you bled upon the bitter tree:
A yard of tinsel ribbon bought and sold;
A paper wreath; a day at home for me.
The merry bells ring out, the people kneel;
Up goes the man of God before the crowd;
With voice of honey and with eyes of steel
He drones your humble gospel to the proud.
Nobody listens. Less than the wind that blows
Are all your words to us you died to save.
O Prince of Peace! O Sharon's dewy Rose!
How mute you lie within your vaulted grave.
The stone the angel rolled away with tears
Is back upon your mouth these thousand years.

From the Toy Box

Nancy Henry

God
they sent me to tell you
none of us can help it.
Can't operate correctly,
can't fly, won't wind up,
can't even make a start
for the tops of those clouds.
So many pieces melted,
bent, skewed, pocked,
utterly undermined with rust.

What we want to know:
when this ends,
how will you decide
which ones of us
are most broken,
how will you choose
which ones of us
to throw away?

Out Here

Robin Merrill

I know why he killed himself.
You know, the old man
who spent thirty years
trying to break out of prison
and his last two
aching to get back in.
I know him, how he missed
that cold comfort of gray.
I too, have seen colors to be scary.
I know why he carved his name
in the headboard at the boarding house
before he swallowed the stolen pills.
For thirty years they barked his name.
He hasn't heard it since. After living
the same day over and over,
regimen and routine,
now he wakes without schedule.
There are no friends here.
There is no family.
He left all of that behind.
Though he didn't know it then,
prison gave him purpose.
It's lonely out here.

Free Agent

Marija Sanderling

He shoots baskets
The empty lot
The netless hoop
Suspended like a halo
His daily routine
Sometimes with others
Mostly alone
To shoot and dribble
Like the players on tv
He's a free agent
Who dropped out of school
So even the gym teacher
Can't tell him
If he's any good.
Three hours a day
No traveling
No transitions
Just free throws and slam dunks
And all it's gotten him
Is a 90% success rate
And a view of the city
Through the chain-link fence.

To the Infinitesimal

Betsy Sholl

I opened a holy book, hoping to find
the part about turning the other cheek,
and out you flew, hovering dot

smaller than a comma, winged inkling.
Were you late when names were given out,
an afterthought, spittle from a cough

at the end of creation? Feeling you
graze my check, I lunged like a clumsy golem,
but you gave me the slip.

How can anything so small have a will,
a want, the wits to flee two clapped hands?
In a time revving for war, with experts

stoking the engines, insisting necessity,
you're a nil, a naught, a nuisance to ignore,
not one of mystery's vexing ellipses. . .

If your wings whir, if you buzz at all,
it's below our hearing, little serif
broken off some word in holy writ

to drift among us, inaudible
argument illustrating creation's
fondness for every last tittle and jot.

Death and the Turtle

May Sarton

I watched the turtle dwindle day by day,
Get more remote, lie limp upon my hand;
When offered food he turned his head away;
The emerald shell grew soft. Quite near the end
Those withdrawn paws stretched out to grasp
His long head in a poignant dying gesture.
It was so strangely like a human clasp,
My heart cracked for the brother creature.

I buried him, wrapped in a lettuce leaf,
The vivid eye sunk inward, a dull stone.
So this was it, the universal grief;
Each bears his own end knit up in the bone.
Where are the dead? we ask, as we hurtle
Toward the dark, part of this strange creation,
One with each limpet, leaf, and smallest turtle —
Cry out for life, cry out in desperation!

Who will remember you when I have gone,
My darling ones, or who remember me?
Only in our wild hearts the dead live on.
Yet these frail engines bound to mystery
Break the harsh turn of all creation's wheel,
For we remember China, Greece, and Rome,
Our mothers and our fathers, and we steal
From death itself rich store, and bring it home.

Nature

Henry Wadsworth Longfellow

As a fond mother, when the day is o'er,
  Leads by the hand her little child to bed,
  Half willing, half reluctant to be led,
  And leave his broken playthings on the floor,
Still gazing at them through the open door,
  Nor wholly reassured and comforted
  By promises of others in their stead,
  Which, though more splendid, may not please him more;

So Nature deals with us, and takes away
  Our playthings one by one, and by the hand
  Leads us to rest so gently, that we go
Scarce knowing if we wish to go or stay,
  Being too full of sleep to understand
  How far the unknown transcends the what we know.

Question in a Field

Louise Bogan

Pasture, stone wall, and steeple,
What most perturbs the mind:
The heart-rending homely people,
Or the horrible beautiful kind?

To an Artist, to Take Heart

Louise Bogan

Slipping in blood, by his own hand, through pride,
Hamlet, Othello, Coriolanus fall.
Upon his bed, however, Shakespeare died,
Having endured them all.

Salt to the Brain

(In Praise of Poets)

David Moreau

As a rule we are not the brain surgeons
or the bridge builders. We did not figure
how to make water flow in a pipe
or keep airplanes stable in flight.
Instead, we stood in a circle and chanted,
"All praise to the most beautiful bridge,"
then walked across it.

As a rule we do not meet the payroll
or keep the factories open.
Others figured how enzymes work
and built hydraulic brakes.
Instead, we were the ones at the machines
whose idea it was to sing, "Happy Birthday,"
or "Nobody Knows the Trouble I've Seen."

In this world the moneychangers change money.
The nurses nurse and the lawyers lawyer.
My mother feeds the stray cats that come
to the screen door of her house in Marion Oaks.
The orange tiger has a nasty scratch.
The poets take note,
add this small pinch of salt to the brain,
our gift to the taste of existence.

Where Inspiration Has Learned a Thing or Two

Mekeel McBride

From the trees because they are the true intuitives.
Palm readers of sunlight and storm, calm interpreters
for any kind of wind, doing most of the detective work
on shooting stars and aurora borealis. Their easy come,
easy go romances with migrating birds scarcely bear
recording and not even the quick cinema jump cuts
from summer to snow bother them. Even if there is snow,
temperature in the minus numbers, something continues
to live, invisible, at the core. Looking at the trees, you might
see in the bare branches only the bones of Babayaga's hand
or the possibility of kindling for your wood stove, owl haven,
or a kind of living elegy blessed on the highest branch
by one thin crow. Of course you could be wrong. What
inspiration looks like is never really what it is.

Spring Thaw

Ruth F. Guillard

Night, early April
White rivers of rain, snowmelt
Roar over the rocks
Scouring the steep slopes
Tripping over grey boulders
Hillsides echoing

Every spring I wait
For this sweet sound of release
The earth rejoicing.

Growing Lettuce

Henry Braun

I have broken soil
and run a line in the blackness with my finger
and dropped the flea-like seeds in
too thickly.

Even so, even so,
the lettuce comes, standing room only,
as a favor to a first try
and is a shy green.

Zones of Peeper

Carl Little

Driving home from a party, parsing
conversations, car windows down
to greet first real summer heat,
we pass through zones of peeper —

not song, not chorus, though
scientists no doubt find pattern
in the high-pitched whatever it is.
Nor peep, which reminds you of

silly chicks falling over each other
in an incubator. Every moist venue
between Pretty Marsh and Somesville,
every hundred yards brings

this antic singing, somewhat
alien in tone, magical too,
like fireflies but auditory,
not synthesized but a perfect

cacophony of the higher ranges,
tiny frogs doing their spring thing,
flinging music into dank milieu
of pond edge and marsh, inspiring

a certain joy in our recap of the evening
as if every fault could be forgiven
when you consider the rest of the world
wild and wet and flipping out.

Fiddleheads

Richard Foerster

Only the first scrolls inscripted
with the long winter's undeciphered
lore, only the tight-harnessed
coils volting up fully
charged from peaty earth would do:

tiny crosiers straining to hook
the sky; spring's furled lace —
wings before the sun had a chance
to spirit them with flight. Arrested

potential I demanded with each
flick of my pruning knife, not
woodland crofts feathered wide
in August with spore-laden tracery.

How the future seemed to lie
there before me, curled and delectable.
Already the virgin oil sizzled
in my mind till I was sure
the skillet would whisper hosannas.

My Hairy Legs

Mariana S. Tupper

My hairy legs say No to sheer pantyhose
accompanied by stiff pumps and hard soles.
No to razors, depilatories and electrolysis.

They resent hours in the bathroom
yanking on fabric strips
and wiping up little hairs in the tub.

My hairy legs take a stand against propriety.

They say Yes to shorts,
Yes please to stockings with crazy stripes.

My hairy legs are happy to wear pants,
and gowns on formal occasions,

though they long for the moment
when the party is over and they can kick up
their heels and feel the wind in their hair.

Spring Cleaning

Ellen M. Taylor

Why are there no poems of the joy
of vacuum cleaning after a long

winter? Of the pleasure of pulling
the couch back, sucking up cobwebs, dead

flies, candy cane wrappers, cookie crumbs?
The sun rises earlier now, flooding

the room with daffodil light, enough
to see long unseen clumps of dog hair,

wood ash, needles from holiday greens.
The vacuum crackles over a spot

of gravelly dirt, until at last
the carpet pile is clean, floorboards gleam.

Then, the bliss when the machine is pressed off,
no sound left but the tick, tick of the clock.

A Parrot

May Sarton

My parrot is emerald green,
His tail feathers, marine.
He bears an orange half-moon
Over his ivory beak.
He must be believed to be seen,
This bird from a Rousseau wood.
When the urge is on him to speak,
He becomes too true to be good.

He uses his beak like a hook
To lift himself up with or break
Open a sunflower seed,
And his eye, in a bold white ring,
Has a lapidary look.
What a most astonishing bird,
Whose voice when he chooses to sing
Must be believed to be heard.

That stuttered staccato scream
Must be believed not to seem
The shriek of a witch in the room.
But he murmurs some muffled words
(Like someone who talks through a dream)
When he sits in the window and sees
To to-and-fro wings of wild birds
In the leafless improbable trees.

Spooked Moose

Douglas Woody Woodsum

Like a real bull in a bullfight, the full-grown moose
Lowered his head and ripped through my neighbor's laundry, pinned
To the line from the house corner to the apple tree.

And like a bride with a twenty-foot train, it dragged the line
And the clothes across my neighbor's lawn, leaving a wake
Of clothespins, jeans, tee shirts, and boxer shorts every few yards.

Then, like a moose in a panic because it has rope
And clothing tangled about its horns and more rope and clothes flapping
About its torso and rear legs, very like such a moose,

It lowered its head again and charged through the old barbed wire
Pasture fence, snapping the rotten fenceposts off at ground level,
Dragging and, finally, snapping, the rusty wires of a forgotten farm.

And then like a fearful beast learning fear for the first time,
It picked up speed as a bedsheet flopped onto its face
and three or four dragging fenceposts barked its rear ankles and shins.

It tripped and fell breaking through the fence again on the far
Side of the field, but struggled up once more to crash
Into the undergrowth and disappear amid the trees.

Lastly, like stunned townspeople in the wake of a twister,
My neighbor and I picked up the strewn pieces of clothing
As we followed tracks, like post-holes, into the dented woods.

New England Asters

Lynn Ascrizzi

They're firing purple from the rock wall,
shouting hurrahs amid gloriosas,
towering on leggy stalks
near the rose trellis, before the frost.

The dames are taking over.
Fringy and sticky, drunk with nectar,
they lean and swagger,
staging a revolution.

Volunteers from last year's seeds
spring up near the house,
and new forces bivouac
down the long dirt drive,
ready to occupy the roadside
past the mailbox.

Shovel in hand, I am fully enlisted
in the cause of late bloomers.
I transplant rootstock,
shake out new progeny,
post ensigns amid the wan and cheerless,
marshal troops down desolate hollows,
seed my universe with stars.

They All Come Back

Sarah Jane Woolf-Wade

The girl who shone in Broadway shows
was born here in the village on Fourth of July
and a Rockette who danced in the chorus line
came back to raise babies ten miles away.

The clamdigger brothers, working two tides a day,
sculpted like statues, left town in their prime.
The doctor brother returned to build homes,
the recovering teacher now fishes the sea.

The stenos, hairdressers, building inspectors
now all snuggle into the arms of the village.
People who married, those who traveled abroad
nestle into the homesteads built by their fathers.

Some born in the town migrate south in the winter,
reappear with songbirds early in spring.
The city-based clerk breathes deep of Maine air
as she crosses the Kittery bridge heading North.

Up on the hill among all the gravestones
lie the man shot dead in a place far from home
and a faraway baby who lived only a day.
Aunt Emma says, as she picks up a stitch,

"Our folks, they all come back in the end."

The Clerks

Edwin Arlington Robinson

I did not think that I should find them there
When I came back again; but there they stood,
As in the days they dreamed of when young blood
Was in their cheeks and women called them fair.
Be sure, they met me with an ancient air, —
And yes, there was a shop-worn brotherhood
About them; but the men were just as good,
And just as human as they ever were.

And you that ache so much to be sublime,
And you that feed yourself with your descent,
What comes of all your visions and your fears?
Poets and kings are but the clerks of Time,
Tiering the same dull webs of discontent,
Clipping the same sad alnage of the years.

Frenchboro

Susan Deborah King

Maybe on an outer island they don't care
as much how things look. Almost nothing
but lobster boats in this narrow harbor
their two-ways blaring into air otherwise pristine.
Very few pleasure craft.
Right by the dock, a wooden hull
collapsed, and is flattening,
boards slowly falling away from each other
like a body flummoxed by exhaustion.
The shed next to it, barely
holding together, windows
punched out, slumps.
Both just left, not cleaned up, built back,
hidden, cleared away or taken apart
and used for kindling.
Weather has made every effort to polish them.
Still, they're duller than tarnished silver.
They've given out, no good anymore,
not even for tuning the wind.
No one here pretends they are
or even gives a hoot.
Why do I find them beautiful?

Washington County, Maine

Tom Sexton

Apple trees heavy with the season's fruit,
piebald, yellow, planet-red, even black,
stand abandoned in fields, the unintended
gift of those who long ago moved on,
a gift to waxwings and even to the tonedeaf
crows in their undertaker's suits,
to the man driving slowly, window down,
to the worms in their snow-white orbit.

By Passamaquoddy Bay

Tom Sexton

Thin light over Campobello Island
to the east when I rise to walk
the long abandoned railroad bed.
Not a trace is left of the rails.
I have several letters to answer
and yesterday's paper to read,
but the wild apples are waiting
cold on the tongue, polished by mist.

Coming Home

Elizabeth Tibbetts

Oh, God, the full-faced moon is smiling at me
in his pink sky, and I'm alive, alive(!)
and driving home to you and our new refrigerator.
A skin of snow shines on the mountain beyond Burger King
and this garden of wires and poles and lighted signs.
Oh, I want to be new, I want to be the girl I saw
last night at the mike, sex leaking from her fingertips
as they traveled down to pick at her hem.
She was younger than I've ever been, with hair cropped,
ragged clothes, and face as clear as a child's.
She read as though she were in bed, eyes half closed,
teeth glistening, her shimmering body written
beneath her dress. She held every man in the audience
taut, and I thought of you. Now I'm coming home
dressed in my sensible coat and shoes, my purse
and a bundle of groceries beside me. When I arrive
we'll open the door of our Frigidaire
to its shining white interior, fill the butter's
little box, set eggs in their hollows, slip meats
and greens into separate drawers, and pause
in the newness of the refrigerator's light
while beside us, through the window,
the moon will lay a sheet on the kitchen floor.

5

What It's Like There

Home

Dawn Potter

So wild it was when we first settled here.
Spruce roots invaded the cellar like thieves.
Skunks bred on the doorstep, cluster flies jeered.
Ice-melt dripped shingles and screws from the eaves.
We slept by the stove, we ate meals with our hands.
At dusk we heard gunshots, and wind and guitars.
We imagined a house with a faucet that ran
From a well that held water. We canvassed the stars.
If love is an island, what map was our hovel?
Dogs howled on the mainland, our cliff washed away.
We hunted for clues with a broken-backed shovel.
We drank all the wine, night dwindled to gray.
    When we left, a flat sunrise was threatening snow,
    But the frost heaves were deep. We had to drive slow.

Eel-Grass

Edna St. Vincent Millay

No matter what I say,
        All that I really love
Is the rain that flattens on the bay,
        And the eel-grass in the cove;
The jingle-shells that lie and bleach
        At the tide-line, and the trace
Of higher tides along the beach:
        Nothing in this place.

Sixty-Five Degrees

Nancy A. Henry

In April,
we hike in from the back orchard
after our winter of white-birch austerity.

All is pandemonium:
frog-muddy boot-sucking swamp earth,
crumblemoss log, shelf-lichen,
salamander, centipede,
snowmelt shadow-hollow,
fly-keening backwoods lowland,
messy fertile celebration
and head-swimming hymn
to spring.

Magic Show

Mariana S. Tupper

It happens here twice a day:
    beds of seaweed levitate a dozen feet
    clamflats vanish
    rivulets of sand pour down like lava
    sparkling flecks of mica swirl like smoke.
When it happens again at night,
    white sand turns black
    moonlight catches on starfish
    phosphorescence floats among the rocks
    wind echoes against the sky.
Then the whole beach disappears,
revealed again when darkness
is swept off like a giant scarf
by the hand of dawn.

Up with Fishermen and Birds

Susan Deborah King

As first light copies from the sky its pink
onto the water, and lobster boats
motor out to drop or pull their traps; as they
swish deftly the long train of their wakes
around buoys bobbing proud, heraldic colors
over the sea's wave-smoothened field;
as captains in orange waders stand at the helms,
or lower traps over the gunwales,
their engines rasping like morning
trying to clear its throat; as deer bow
in an attitude of worship into the mist
hovering just above the meadow,
their backs caught tawny in the rising light;
as bees make their gold-gathering rounds
of poppies, balm and mallow; as crows
harangue each other; as the hummingbird whirrs
to probe the fuchsia for its breakfast juice;
as the phoebe keeps putting its name
before the world, and the morning glory
composes itself in the shadows waiting
for a spotlight before it blows its horn zenith blue –
in this hour, the poet, too, is alert
in her cerulean chair on the porch.
Binoculars handy, books stacked around her,

she bears witness to the beginning, embellishing
the fresh, clean pages of the day with words of praise
that we have once again come whole, come new
out of the dark, out of the dark.

The Saint of Returnables

Elizabeth Tibbetts

Our saint of returnables is back, riding, slow
mile after mile, along the spring roadside,
baskets strapped to his old bike, plastic bags
hung from the handlebars. His gaze averts
to the ditch as he watches for what glitters,
each bottle and can he picks a nickel towards
sustenance. He pedals March through November,
through good and God-awful weather, claiming
what's been tossed out or lost until his bike
is as packed as a mule. When he glances up
we see his face full-on, a face expression
has been erased from, so he looks as though
he has lost his own story somewhere down the road.
But what looks simple could be a twisting path
that would lead to a man's heart. Not the tough
muscle pumping spring air into his thighs, but
that imagined space of the soul, where he stores
everything, and watches, and waits for what's
to come. Yet we're already done, having driven fast
past him—past wood frogs' muttering talk
and blackbirds' red-winged flashes in alders,
past swatches of witch grass and day lilies, leaves
so fierce they push up green inches every day.

Peonies

Robert Siegel

In June these
globes of white flame
swell, explosions so very
slow, we see in them absolute
fire at the center, stasis
of star's core,

or a fragile
moonglow distilled
ghostly in each alembic.
From their green ambush these
unearthly aliens assault
us with color

for a week
then gradually fade
into another dimension. As
Dante saw the stars in a glass,
a corolla of souls,
each reflecting

the other's light
and charity, so in these
low white spheres we contemplate
mirroring heavens, petals, tongues
stammering silent music from
one root of fire.

Summer Episcopalians

(notes from an introvert)

Thomas R. Moore

They are more self-confident than I,
and even though I'm one of them,

they rattle me when I overhear their spiels
in deli about imported Swiss before

choosing Champagne Brie, or when
the women, white-haired, blue-blooded,

chat so self-assuredly in coffee and tea,
their crisp tennis dresses showing

their pedigree with baskets full of organic
pears, natural chicken thighs,

and English breakfast tea. The men
are clean-shaven with jaws that say

prominent, sailing tans melding
into winter's Merlot seas. Their

faces are almost names. I dodge
into canned vegetables and flee.

A Piano at Evening

Thomas Carper

Il étonne lentement.
(He astonishes slowly.)
– *Baudelaire, on the paintings of Corot*

The music she's performing, while the sun
Sinks down, comes softly through an open door
Into the evening calm, and has begun
Altering all we thought we'd known before.
The bushes by the porch, a dusty green
Throughout the inattentions of the day,
Now look more deeply colored, with a sheen
That glimmers as we pause to hear her play.
And now the fine proportions of a tree
Are vivid. While arpeggios declare
Her mastery of the difficult, we see
New symmetries, as vistas everywhere
By slow astonishment are rearranged.
We walk on toward a growing darkness, changed.

Villanelle for the Pond

Peter Harris

We gather at the pond so we can praise
not art but trees, water, echoing sky.
The cast arrives at five, never the same,

three or four or five of us a day,
plus a dock, swallows, a hawk. Turtles lie
on rocks at the pond's edge as if for praise.

This is not music or poetry, not the sway
of work, but the sway of water, trees close by.
This cast arrives at five, never the same.

One swims straight for the dam, another dallies
by the dock, another sidestrokes away quietly.
We gather at the pond so we can praise.

Some bring grief; others are just dazed.
The pond's an alchemist. The pond is kind.
The cast arrives at five, grows sane.

Each week, someone new, from away.
Each week, another someone says goodbye.
We gather at the pond so we can praise.
The cast departs at six, never the same.

Appointment

Candice Stover

Not that it knows my name
or that I call it
any name at all—

pond, refuge, sanity, little jewel . . .

Not that it knows I approach it
summer mornings
like a lover

I undress for without hesitating—
sandals on the bank,
towel draping the branches,

welcoming even the sharp stones
it passes over
like certain betrayals…

how I lie on my side and let
the cool of its skin
brush my cheek, float

my body, this surface
where the loon also learns
how to cry for its species

and where stems of bladderwort rise
above the ugliness
of our name for it:

those delicate carnivores
I am not afraid to swim near
with their beautiful open mouths.

Island Transport

Elizabeth Garber

Just off the long granite-bermed dock
the wheelbarrows wait under birch shade
in feathery grasses. They are beamy,
like oxen flicking their tails, ready
to haul with hand-hewn oak handles,
hammered leg braces, and oiled axles.

Hours after summer people propelled them,
loaded and wobbly, across the island,
they have settled beside the Big House.
The wheelbarrows are painted sky blue,
aqua, salmon, like cheerful aprons with
roomy pockets. Wide-hipped, they linger
like chatting aunts. They would shuck corn
or snip peas off the back porch if they could.

In the Pasture

Kate Barnes

It would be impossible to draw these three workhorses
without a pencil of light
as they stand broadside to the afternoon sun
outlined with narrow lines of fire around their vast
chestnut forms, almost black against the dazzle.
The young mare swings her long tail from hip to hip,
and her Titian-blond mane hangs over her shoulder
like the ringletted chevelure of a Victorian belle,
innocent and alluring.
                                        Beyond her
the two big geldings, brothers and team mates,
scratch each other's wide red backswith careful incisors.
                                        Swallows fly
over the grass, cloud shadows cross the lake
and darken the blue of the hills on the opposite shore
but in the pasture the sun is shining,
the afternoon wind has driven off the flies,
and the three big horses are all at their ease;
a small, happy society
of souls who are gentle and do no harm,
who live in God's pocket, who spend the long summer days
moving from sunshine to shade and back to the sun,
who want nothing but to be where they are.

July Storm

Elizabeth Coatsworth

Like a tall woman walking across the hayfield
the rain came slowly, dressed in crystal and the sun.
Rustling along the ground, she stopped at our apple tree
only for a whispering minute, then swept darkening
skirts over the lake,
and so serenely climbed the wooden hills.
Was the rainbow a ribbon that she wore?
We saw it when she was gone. It seemed a part of her brightness
and the way she moved lightly, but with assurance,
over the earth.

From Cadillac Mountain

Elizabeth Coatsworth

So might a Chinese sage have seen the world,
seen mist and humpbacked islands from a mountain,
with a hawk hanging in a silver sky.
So might a Chinese sage have seen his heart
and its tranquility shown in elements
of earth, sky, water, the only fire
white fire of the sun. Here the wind
has come from far away, unhurriedly
traveling from plains and forests, nameless lakes
to seek the ocean and new hemispheres.
The mind, stiffened with routine, stretches, floats
off with the mist, off with the quiet wind
to undefined horizons of its own.

Glacial Erotic

Carl Little

When the great sheet of ice lifted,
enormous boulders were left scattered
on mountainsides and deep in the forests.
They assumed unusual positions.

One massive example, with a smooth top
and curved sides, served as the trysting place
for lovers from the town of Bar Harbor.
They assumed unusual positions.

You say erratic, I say erotic, let's call
the whole thing rock. And when the glaciers
next return, flipping us over in our beds,
we, too, will assume most unusual positions.

The Great Rock in the Woods

Henry Braun

for Matty Goodman

It sees nothing where it has been seen
by all eyes in the climax forests
that pass in slow succession after fires.
Even the white bear may have known it
glazed by the last touch of the glacier
that, miles away, broke it off the mountain.
The story of its roll down here
to this surprising presence,
its ride with the field of stones
that made Maine hard to farm, and again hard,
is soon told.
      I take this boulder for a landmark
and pass by
in the deep woods on my road to friends.

Rock Maples

Megan Grumbling

By other names, these trees seem sweeter yet;
this older one's an homage to the strength
ringing its bird's-eye grain, this best beloved
of maples, generous in sap and hue.
So near to an ideal, its silhouette.
Above the trunk, full branches grant a broad
ascension, then resolve oval relief.
A beautiful shape that that's got, you see.

Dimensions lower Booker's voice, distilled
this strong by symmetry designed, it seems,
to let the eye go idle in delight.
That maple's shape persuades vision to yield
to the gestalt of the beheld, inscribed
at once to us, unbidden, crimson, plain.
The ease becomes the image in the tree,
an order to alight upon, not seek.

The Berwick Cemetery holds it, sure
in waiting stone: this tree above his name
where one date soon now balances with new,
to crown the natural order. Soon, it comes.
The shape of it. It's perfect, Booker rules,
to look at what the shape of that tree is.
All maple branches crest, as arcs will meet
when this blank rock turns graven, and complete.

Shopping Together

Robert Siegel

Cardboard stars crowd the shelves,
and moons marked off a penny,
as you glide, standing on the cart,

to a touch in any direction.
We shine in a dusk of eggplants,
sleepy with a perfume of apples,

wander forests of asparagus,
drift in a green ocean
of lettuce, avocados, celery,

down an avalanche of oranges
to a wilderness of bananas—
an El Dorado of lavish aromas.

Still, beyond the parsley are berries
superfluous with juice
that break in our mouths like old sorrows,

and melons like a school of whales
shouldering a cool secret
over the edge of the world.

All the way home, bags leaning
lovesick against us,
we feed each other plums and dark cherries.

September Staying

Patricia Ranzoni

The air is made of missing:
spaces where you were, sounds
lacking yours. A robin basks
on the arbor appreciating as much
as I, and whole bubbles of butterflies
bounce in the garden quiet but for
crickets nearby, crows far off,
leaves high up. Certain flies buzz
somewhere. The spider still weaves
in the hops vine but hummingbirds
have gone, like summerfolk, like you,
to other worlds leaving hardy ones
to season ourselves in stillness again
to find our own peace. Our own place.

From *Under Mount Blue*

Henry Braun

Reading Late

Some evenings fragility
lays itself out on roads
from the novel you are reading,
old peculiar enlargements
that keep you wakeful
long after the book closes.
Someone was alive
whom you followed by oil lamp
for hours through the pages
and now, in a quiet house,
everyone breathing must be looked at
and more than looked at,
accompanied.

Firewood Sermon

Sticks of wood are personalities
like dogs and cats, but simpler.
One hisses with the rain
garnered slowly on a woodpile. One
cackles cackles groans
and falls to its side.
Two, brought near strike up an acquaintance
in the burning world.

Crossing the Blueberry Barrens

Tom Sexton

No one else was on the road when
We drove across the blueberry barrens
Glowing like wind-blown embers.
We gleaned berries from the edges
Of fields raked by migrant workers
Who had moved on into Nova Scotia.
Glaciers had scraped the land to the bone.
Dusk came on. Ground fog moved in.
Boulders rose like the prows of ships,
Their long oars muffled and steady,
Then the narrow road began to descend
To a small river town's empty main street
That was as dark and as wet as a seal.

Vespers

Theodore Enslin

That time in the early evening,
a cold sunset gone —
colder than I remember
a year ago
        at apparently
the same time —
the time when cars
go by, one after another.
Purposeful, not speeding,
just to get home.
My neighbors are tired
and hungry
                    For what
do they hunger
beyond a break in the day,
in from the cold?
                    A warm dinner.
What more do they want?
Where do they turn?
Words fail.
They cannot tell me.
If they could
I would not hear them
going past
                    down
this ordinarily quiet road.

Snow-Flakes

Henry Wadsworth Longfellow

Out of the bosom of the Air,
  Out of the cloud-folds of her garments shaken,
Over the woodlands brown and bare,
  Over the harvest-fields forsaken,
    Silent, and soft, and slow
    Descends the snow.

Even as our cloudy fancies take
  Suddenly shape in some divine expression,
Even as the troubled heart doth make
  In the white countenance confession,
    The troubled sky reveals
    The grief it feels.

This is the poem of the air,
  Slowly in silent syllables recorded;
This is the secret of despair,
  Long in its cloudy bosom hoarded,
    Now whispered and revealed
    To wood and field.

Splitting Wood in Winter

Douglas Woodsum

You'll need a barn with a big door, the old-fashioned
kind that hangs on wheels, slides open
down a track. You'll need a bare bulb, the sun
having sunk before your return from work.
You'll need a splitting maul (the ax always
gets stuck), a medieval weapon perfect
for pillaging heat from the heart of hardwood.
You can plug in the portable radio
or just listen to the hush of the swing,
then thwack . . . or thoonk, the soft clinks or cloonks
of the splits falling from the chopping block
onto the old, thick, scarred floorboards of the barn.
You'll need your hands to rip apart pieces
still connected by strips of unsplit wood.
You'll need to load the canvas carrier
thrice, enough to survive the dead of night.
You won't need reminding, "Splitting wood warms
you twice: once cutting it, once burning it."
You'll smile walking through the cold, back to the house,
your hot breath a harbinger of wood smoke.

Starting the Subaru at Five Below

Stuart Kestenbaum

After 6 Maine winters and 100,000 miles,
when I take it to be inspected

I search for gas stations where they
just say beep the horn and don't ask me to

put it on the lift, exposing its soft
rusted underbelly. Inside is the record

of commuting: apple cores, a bag from
McDonald's, crusted Dunkin' Donuts cups,

a flashlight that doesn't work and one
that does, gas receipts blurred beyond

recognition. Finger tips numb, nose
hair frozen, I pump the accelerator

and turn the key. The battery cranks,
the engine gives 2 or 3 low groans and

starts. My God it starts. And unlike
my family in the house, the job I'm

headed towards, the poems in my briefcase,
the dreams I had last night, there is

no question about what makes sense.
White exhaust billowing from the tail pipe,

heater blowing, this car is going to
move me, it's going to take me places.

6

What the Creatures Say

Fugue

Thomas Carper

Perhaps the birds first taught it, their *ta-wee*
Repeating while they soared, with every bird
Performing calls and cries unfailingly
In what seemed freedom. This was overheard
As pattern from a singing sweep of sky;
Then lengthened, varied, twittered with a trill;
Then given darker tone to multiply
The implications of the tune until
The listener who noted every note,
Who heard each harmony, could overhear,
Before the breath fell silent in the throat,
Music beyond the limit of the ear,
Music with every moment moving toward
Complete fulfillment in a final chord.

Three Poems About Birds

Marnie Reed Crowell

Peek

Between the twigs
a warbler sings

morning air
aglow with aria

and all I see
is a tiny eye.

Haiku by Sparrow

Pale sun, old snow
   white-throated sparrow
cold pure call of spring
call of spring

Spotted Sandpiper

Just at the silver seam
between the sea and shore
spotted sandpiper
teeters, speaks softly to itself
a poem it has by heart.

Miss Shrew

Gary Rainford

It's a chill morning in May.
I follow Meri, whirling and speechless, to a nook
underneath the staircase.

Trapped inside a jar
a velvety shrew, smaller than my big toe,
is dying, but holding to life
like petals of roses to a cut stem.

When I palm the jar, tiny shrew feet struggle,
then fall. And when she lifts her head,
her red eyes close.

Meri feels so terrible we let Miss Shrew go loose
way out back by the honeysuckle vines
in the mice and shrew hotel
of tall grasses.

"I want Miss Shrew to live, see another sunrise,"
Meri points tearfully at the sky.

"Go shrew, go shrew, go," I say, down on my knees
and elbows, praying for a twitch
of hope, but she hardly moves.

About Bees is What I Say Aloud When You Ask What I'm Thinking

Kimberly Cloutier Green

Watching bees plunge into sunlit blossoms
and stagger back besotted
   by the apple nectar on their tongues,
I feel their hunger as mine—

         the longing to linger awhile
as though winged,
   looped in this daze of pink light, confusing
morning for a flower,
   all my drowsy preparations
of our toast and tea
   a slow, zigzagging industry,

         then sharing my stores
of gathered sweetness with you
   in a rapture of emptying,
each turn I make in my dance
   timed for the signal flashes of gold
dust on my feet on my hands on your face.

On Wanting Only One Thing

Rachel Contreni Flynn

for Patrick

This morning the hooded merganser
appears lazy on the lake, puckered feet tucked
beneath her rump so she's just coasting,
just carving with the cargo of her body

a sloppy channel through snake grass,
silent as a handbag. The merganser pays
no attention to kites swooping in the spruce,
loons keening in the coves, or cormorants

airing their wings on the shore. The merganser
never swivels her head for sleep or grief
or even grooming, so it seems she might be stupid
or nearly dead. But then, at the bright twist

of fin beneath her, her soul becomes a syringe.
She unhinges her joints into sleek steel,
plunges through cold water, small heart soaring,
mind clenched behind hopeful, topaz eyes.

Listening for Loons

Gary Lawless

i

wild roses down
to the water
one loon alone
northeast of the island
cedarscent

ii

water lily or
loon white
on the water both
bright
flowers flowers
on the surface of
this world

iii

like loons we dive under
dive under and
come up somewhere else

iv

every night now
i listen for loons
to hear their voices
to leave this body
to return to stars

Mockingbird

Mekeel McBride

The mockingbird's a live encyclopedia
of song, Listen, it can be
the whole world humming to itself:
tinsel consonant of wind
in love with whatever its silken glove
touches, never touches,

and then again it's just the normal chatter
of thrust or grackle.
The mockingbird's own song? Difficult
to hear in this aria that includes
news from every absent bird,
but slightly richer. All night

it stays awake, slipping its glad opera
into the delicate bone cage
of the Emperor's or your sleeping
ear. For this, the glass blower wakes
and weeps, knowing how frail his world is
and imperfect.

At the Birdfeeder

Richard Foerster

My neighbor's cat, all nimble
traipse and jig in his fur tuxedo,
eyes a panicked chickadee in its own
fancy dress. A squall of black

millet seeds peppers the snowcrusted
ground, where the cat freezes,
gazing toward paradise, his entire being now
hellbent on that one morsel. The bird,

though frantic flutter, is no less consumed
with want. It's somehow managed to slip
inside the feeder, trapped itself within
that glass house of miraculous plenty,

wanting nothing but escape, while the cat
squats beneath that dwindling spillage,
content to remain there forever, if he must,
exiled with his exquisite desire.

Brothers

Robert P. Tristram Coffin

Now with my lamp I make a little world
And sit inside it like a jealous god.
The small creatures of the night come to my pane
And peer at me and know that I am good,
Their eyes fill up with worship and their fear,
They think of me somehow as their lost sun
And flex their paper wings and make them sing
The very minute hymns they make in flight,
They beat like small, quick hearts against my glass.

I wish I were the wonder that has lit
Their round, cool eyes, or knew some way to tell them
That they and I are brothers in the dark.

To a Garden Spider

Leslie Moore

Dangling over the zucchini like a dangerous jewel,
you set up housekeeping amid the gladioli,
your silken web spanning stiff green blades,
and you, poised in its eye, alert to possibilities,
a black face silhouetted in yellow horror.

Below, squash bugs swarm the zucchini
leaving fat leaves in ashen heaps. I pluck
one from the horde and drop it onto your web.
Its six black feet catch fast in the interstices.
Your reaction is unequivocal.

A ripple of legs carries you to your victim.
You cradle it in your eight-fold embrace.
A swaddling in shrouds from your spinnerets,
one paralyzing kiss, then you leave your prey
dangling to retake your silent center.

Your web is eloquent—a Charlotte's web.
You write words with your artistry.
And what lessons, I wonder, would you teach me
about solitude and survival? What could I learn
from your deadly attention to detail?

After the Splash

Leslie Moore

We step to the porch railing—
wine glasses in hand, Scrabble forgotten—

to spy a bird floundering in the cove,
dashing the sea with great, feathered
downbeats, almost obscured by the spray.
It's a bald eagle and my heart thrashes with it.

I'm ready to canoe to the rescue,
my husband paddling, me leaning
over the bow, poised to pluck a frantic,
flapping, full-grown eagle out of the sea
in my bare arms. Its wing span is wider
than I am tall, its beak a scimitar.

But the bald eagle doesn't need me.
It settles onto the water, plump as a duck,
turns beak to shore, scoops the sea with
feathery palms, and climbs out on a rocky
shelf, dragging in one talon a fish,
huge and silvery in the sunlight.

Strauss and Cows of Ireland

Mekeel McBride

From my room at dusk I watch
the cows in their late graze.
Great clouds of gnats hang over
them, gauzy as a bride's bouquet.
Downstairs, a radio.
Soprano's aria swells
so delicate and pure
it must be unrequited love
but just what the opera is
I can't tell from here,
though later learn: Strauss,
Der Rosenkavalier.
Cows continue to drift
the dusky pasture, luminous,
as if fed on candlelight
instead of grass. They pass
with heavy gentleness, now
and then stopping to lean toward
our windows with little regard
for human arias that reach them
though it conducts
through me a sweetness:
distant opera and the wandering
of star-tiaraed cows in darkness.

Ants

Lynn Ascrizzi

This morning, after last night's
thunderstorms and torrents of rain,
I watch black ants hurry along
damp boards, on the open porch.

I love their hasty, stop-and-go
movements, how they hug and kiss
each other, antennae
to antennae, as they meet.

I used to think it served biology only—
this habit of touching feelers—
just a simple relay of tribal codes,
a way to broadcast top headlines
of Colony News, with up-to-the-minute
stories of "fatals" on thorny stems,
obits on moles and grasshoppers,
toad alerts and forecasts of frost.

But now, I see their mutual affection,
the joy in each wired greeting,
how each belongs to each
and to the whole, how communicating
is part of love—how love
loves to communicate.

The Dragonfly

Louise Bogan

You are made of almost nothing
But of enough
To be great eyes
And diaphanous double vans;
To be ceaseless movement,
Unending hunger,
Grappling love.

Link between water and air,
Earth repels you.
Light touches you only to shift to iridescence
Upon your body and wings.

Twice-born, predator,
You split into the heat.
Swift beyond calculation or capture
You dart into the shadow
Which consumes you.

You rocket into the day.
But at last, when the wind flattens the grasses,
For you, the design and purpose stop.

And you fall
With the other husks of summer.

Where the Deer Were

Kate Barnes

It's always hard to form a true picture
of what's happening, isn't it?
Difficult to know what's what.

For instance,
the moving tenderness of the desiring man,
the gentle vanity of the desired woman
sliding their bare arms together
in the grass across the stream.
It's late summer,
a misty day, but warm.

I can't see their faces.
So what is happening, really?
Perhaps they are fighting—very evenly.
Perhaps those sounds are groans of pain.
Now the mist
closes my eyes.

When it lifts once more,
I see nothing over there
but a hollow in the long grass
like the places where deer have been lying,
and the only thing I hear
is shallow water making excuses to stone.

Wild Swans

Edna St. Vincent Millay

I looked in my heart while the wild swans went over.
And what did I see I had not seen before?
Only a question less or a question more;
Nothing to match the flight of wild birds flying.
Tiresome heart, forever living and dying,
House without air, I leave you and lock your door.
Wild swans, come over the town, come over
The town again, trailing your legs and crying.

Coydog

Rachel Contreni Flynn

When I look at you,
my life, my eyes
grow lighter, become
a golden coydog's.

I cannot touch you
enough and already
have learned not to try
to trap or tame you,

not even to untangle
your hair. It is enough
that the look of you
lightens me

until I could run
the fields behind our house,
twisting and yipping
with joy.

The Pet

Constance Hunting

O say see
look at my
little monkey
she so puzzled and charming
with that almost human frown

she sits in her
little chair
at her little table
she holds a pen
she is writing

making strange
marks on the white
petalled paper
I am very proud
of her

she is coming
along very nicely
but sometimes
chatters more
than I prefer

and would tear up the page
chew it to bits
did I not interfere
always calmly and stroke
her down

Night Out

Paul Nelson

Blank by the fire.
Coals dropped in platelets. My hands glowed,
years fused. So I got up and drove out the forest road
as if I were a star beneath the jittery stars,
swarming the mountainous sofas.

Thirty below, 2 A.M., I missed the turn beyond the bridge,
slid once around, hallucinated into a drift.
The hood popped. The engine-well filled with snow.
I hadn't been drinking but sat there
thinking how the beauty of that night would freeze in my eyes.
It was then the moose came from the trees, wading,
waving its great, palmated rack, looming above the car.
It looked in, lowered its neck, hooked the rocker panel
and with something of a moan flipped me over, out of the snow,
into the middle of the road, snorted and walked off upside down.
I sat on my neck. I couldn't see the sky,
was wondering, sorry when the headlights came,
the Atlantic Seafood truck for Portland, turning me yellow,
a yolk in a racked egg, almost running me over.
He jimmied the door. I spilled out talking.
He wouldn't believe me any more than you,
how I'd been saved, that my life had been in danger.
The tracks were gone in powder. All-State
looked at the buckled roof but would not call it
and act of God or Man, wouldn't swallow Moose.
But that big, sad face, rubber-lipped above me,
moons in my dreams.

Dog in Winter

Dawn Potter

Up the boggy headland, frozen now, where a stone fence
Submerged in snow and earth-sink hints at pasture
So long vanished that the woods are convinced
Grassland never existed, two bodies climb — one fast,
Black, doe-agile; one slogging and foot-bound
Like a superannuated tortoise. Guess which is me.
Easy to badmouth my grace but oddly hard to expound
On the postcard beauties of our workaday scenery —
Giant pines draped with frosting, wisp of chimney cloud
Threading skyward, and behind the frosted window
A glorious wall of books, lamp-lit; a dear bowed head.
In tales, common enchantment always merits less than woe,
    And perhaps I should collapse on the stoop like a starved Jane Eyre,
    Pleading heat and mercy. But I earn my joy. I mean, I live here.

Coyotes

Leslie Moore

They hug the margins of fields,
slip into creases between trees,
glide across gravel roads at dawn or dusk,
bellies close to the ground, tails
trailing. We hardly know they are here, think
all of this is ours — the property, the shorefront,
the view — until moonless nights
when a choir of coyotes sings to the stars
and one paces the length of our driveway
leaving tracks in the snow and scat
where the dog and I are sure to find it.

7

A Journey of One

Inside the Stone

Kate Barnes

Up in the woods,
in the circle among the beech trees,
last winter one of the lumber horses split a stone
horizontally, with a clip of his big steel shoe.
It had seemed to be a plain gray stone,
but when it was opened a black wall appeared,
rusty at the edges, flecked with pale checks
like unknown constellations, and over all
floated wisps of blue-gray, trailing feathers of clouds.

I brush away the fallen leaves
and stare into the distance inside the stone.
If one could become a bird —
if one could fly into that night —
if one could see the circling of those stars —

and then the woods become very still,
and beech leaves blur at the edge of my vision.
I find I am bending lower and lower.

My Father, My Hands

Richard Blanco

My father gave me these hands, fingers
inch-wide and muscular like his, the same
folds of skin like squinted eyes looking
back at me whenever I wash my hands
in the kitchen sink and remember him
washing garden dirt off his, or helping
my mother dry the dishes every night.

These are his fingernails — square, flat —
ten small mirrors I look into and see him
signing my report card, or mixing batter
for our pancakes on Sunday mornings.
His same whorls of hair near my wrists,
magnetic lines that pull me back to him
tying my shoelaces, pointing at words
as I learned to read, and years later:
greasy hands teaching me to change
the oil in my car, immaculate hands
showing me how to tie my necktie.

These are his knuckles — rising, falling
like hills between my veins — his veins,
his pulse at my wrist under the watch
he left for me ticking since his death,
alive when I hold another man's hand

and remember mine around his thumb
through the carnival at Tamiami Park,
how he lifted me up on his shoulders,
his hands wrapped around my ankles
keeping me steady above the world, still.

No Child of Earthly Kitchens

Mekeel McBride

I owned no raincoat and in the season of storms
was sent to school under my mother's umbrella.

It was the color of pale sherry. The ivory handle
kept about it the faint smell of perfumed wrists.

It never carried me away although I wished it
often enough that I can still see beneath me

people with their umbrellas like black morning glories
growing small on a polished street.

And I see, too, my house as tidy as the shoebox
for a hurt bird; the flat horizon

filling out as purple and plump as an eggplant.
And when the dark arc of the umbrella sets me down

and when my feet again touch stubborn ground
I am no longer a child of earthly kitchens

but find the geometry of clouds closeted in my heart
and in my hair, the strange blue perfume of storm.

Between Stars

Martin Steingesser

In between stars, what distances, and yet, how much vaster
the distance we learn from what is right here.
— Rainer Maria Rilke, Sonnets to Orpheus

When they sent me away for the summer
at four, the journey itself felt like a year.
Mornings it was make the bed, swab the toilet bowl,
sweep floors. After, we assembled in ragged lines,
each a team with an animal name, like cubs
or tadpoles. A counselor wearing a whistle on a cord
called out activities: softball, swim . . .
He'd blow the whistle, and everyone ran to one.
I would turn, walk off into some nearby woods,
lose myself all morning. It's a wonder
no one missed me. At least, no one came looking.
Don't ask what I did. What I remember is the glow —
every moment, leaf and grass blade, every stone,
sunlight scattered among them, patches
of white fire. My heart hummed, more home
lost in woods than I have ever felt—
unless you count the territories of poems
I'm called to write, in which I lose myself,
not unlike the way I wandered those woods.
I might as easily been walking among galaxies,
green distances between leaves endless as stars.
My own certain way—maybe where poetry began
for me, before thinking, before knowing, speechless
in the green world where I wanted to stay.

Fishing

Martin Steingesser

Sometimes words come hard — they resist me
till I pluck them from deep water like hooked fish...
— Lu Ji (261-303)

You have to be willing
to wait days and days with nothing
biting.
          Wait

while the far leaves, the sky change
blues and greens, and birdcalls,
wind, river become the sound of thinking.
This line you cast
                    reaches into different music.

A murmur flutters over the water —
                    be more still . . .

Sometimes a moment happens
                              when what moves

doesn't, when the trees and grasses
along the riverbank seem to hold their breath,
and it is the stones that breathe . . .

                    The fish you want
is rising in another world.

Some Kind of Hunter

Megan Grumbling

He coaxed a pregnant woman right across
the river, and it weren't no easy bridge.
A cousin of an in-law, broke as dirt,
she come up visiting from Vermont too poor
to buy a license. Booker paid it, set
a rifle in her hands, and took her up
to Perkinstown, the brook side, where they come
upon this bridge, just beams and cables, rough.
Full six months big, a borrowed gun; to her,
that span, it looked like one hell of a stunt
when Booker brought her up to it, said, Look,
you've gotta cross that river on them wires.
Now, Booker's gone these routes, matters of course,
for quite a while, and spares no care or feat —
hauls moose out of the woods in split canoes,
checks hoofprints in the gravel pit's pale sand
most every morning, seeing where they cross.
A deer makes no more noise than shadow does,
he told his novice kin, and knows the sound
by going over into silence, deep, and back,
more than a couple times. So when he led
this woman, large with child, up to the bridge,
and she replied, Oh no — I can't do that,
he tried to make her see the other side.
You gotta, Booker said, or else what kind
of hunter are you? Well, that settled things.

Their bridge stretched lean but held, across the way.
She took hold of the cables, hand to steel,
and cradling that gun close, she went across.

Worry Bone

Gibson Fay-LeBlanc

Woke gnawing its remains. Air
the brackish tinge of depths I had

all night been swimming in. No bird
song from the vine-covered fence

my room looks out on — not even
the pigeons' manic calls. I talked

myself down from the bed, a loft,
took paper in trade for the splintered

bone — human or animal
I don't know. I'd picked it clean though,

chewed the joint, cracked one end,
sucked the marrow. Tell me,

Mind, why you ravaged this limb-part.
Tell me what its owner told you in the dark.

The Nots

Gibson Fay-LeBlanc

A writer is accountable also for what
he chooses not to write.
— Edmond Jabés

I haven't described the flight path of my shouts
at two toddlers in a car. I've said little

of my father, a dash. I've not been head
in hands, unable to stop my baby's wails.

That wasn't me, slack-jawed before a screen,
vacant as neon, forgetting my own name.

Not once have I forgotten my son
on his birthday or how to touch my wife.

That was someone else who tightened
your heart with a skate key. Confessed not

being the cherry atop a Manhattan,
nor a tiny umbrella crinkling over a daiquiri.

No tantrums on or off the page.
I told none of the stories I wished to.

They turned out to be tangles of nerve fibers
unjoined, two roads without a bridge between.

I've not spread my arms wide as they would
and said, *Do with me what you will.*

Alms

Betsy Sholl

Small as a fly bump, the little voice
behind me calling Miss, Miss, wanted
a dollar, maybe for food as she said

in that voice of mist, so plaintive
and soft it could have come from inside
my own head, a notch below whisper,
voice of pocket lint, frayed button hole,

voice of God going gnat small. I shivered
and stopped. I looked for the source,
and there it was again, Miss, so slight

it wobbled moth-like on air,
up from a bare trash-filled recess
beside the post office steps. Yes,
I gave the dollar. But I had seven

in my wallet, so clearly that voice
wasn't small enough, still someone
else's sorrow, easy to brush off,

till later that night, in bed, I heard it
again, smaller — miss, miss, little fly strafe
troubling sleep — not a name at all,
but a failure, a lack, a lost chance.

Will We Survive?

Peter Harris

Maybe if we all become that second baseman
who sprinted right, dove, snagged the grounder,
thudded to a stop, too late to get up and change
hands, too late to do anything but what he could
not do, had never tried, could not have done if he had tried:
shovel the gloved ball backhanded over his back,
without looking, to the shortstop. No,
not to the shortstop, but to where the shortstop
would be when he flew across the bag,
barehanded the ball, toed the bag, swiveled,
elevated above the spikes-up, take-out slide,
high enough to make the throw
to first for the double play. Game over.
The not-doable, done. No sound at all inside
the redundant thunder of applause.

Ode to Popcorn

Peter Harris

I pour the shape-shifters
out of the old Mason jar into the pan.
The color of honey, sleek
in their pile of steamlined sibs,
not one of them cares if they're on top,
no rivalries, no grasping,
nothing falsified from skin to core,
no hint about what's pent inside
their quarter inch of seed,
that only gets expressed
when, as now, they're being boiled in oil.

Soon they'll snap the strappings of their haiku form,
explode ten times their size,
go wild, expressionist; no two the same:
fist, cloud, snapdragon, cauliflower,
elephant man, barnacle, meringue, a bowl
of almost weightless meteors,
an orchestra of mutant trumpets
all playing off-white tunes, although,
in each, their husk remains, in caves
or sunk in sockets like weird eyes.

For flakes like these, no way back
to raindrop symmetry. A little salt and butter,
then on to meet their call: to melt
in mouths that crave a hint of paradise.

Doing Time

Betsy Sholl

They call me Babe and make a kissing noise
from inside their bars and inside their rage.
Most of them are men, though they act like boys

who've played too hard and broken all their toys.
Now they're trying to break their metal cage.
They yell out Babe, make that loud kissing noise

as if their catcalls mean they have a voice
routines and bells can't break. "It's just a phase,"
their parents must have said when they were boys.

Don't ask what they're in for; let them enjoy
their small audience, their short time on stage:
"Hey, Babe, how about" — then that kissing noise.

In class they want to rhyme, their way to destroy
all evidence of anguish on the page.
They can't bear to remember being boys.

Some study law, some use another ploy,
daydreaming they'll do time, but never age.
"Hey, Babe," means "kiss off" to that cellblock noise,
to broken men, in here since they were boys.

Stunned

David Sloan

At ten, nothing beat holding my breath
to bursting. In bed with eyes shut,
ears plugged, I'd vanish, sink like a diver
into bottomless inky waters,

and listen below the silence —
long pause of a sea god's breathing —
for that surging thrum, shh-dum
shh-dum shh-dum shh-dum

those fingers drumming on a hidden hull,
steady as a string of bubbles. Later
I loped along mountain roads
loose-limbed, aqua-lunged, Olympian.

At times, when breath and blood converged
and beat in perfect two/four time, I floated
out of my shoes, sh-dum, sh-dum,
made the stretched skin of the sky my ocean.

Now I can't hold a long note without gasping.
My tangled heart flops like a fish
reeled out of the sea, stunned into stillness
between thrashings, bewildered

by its sudden weight and a hard bottom.

What Now, Praying?

Kimberly Cloutier Green

Heart, you softy, you sap — you're getting fat,
breaking into dumbfounded tears in your sleep
and waking bedazzled by ordinary light,
the old cat in a heap of dreams beside you.

There was a time I hardly knew you
were there — thin as air! —
cool customer, smart answer.

Now you babble like a fool,
you're a thief in my throat —
I can't tell anymore where joy gives way
to grief and grief to joy.

Sack in my chest, common store of wishbones,
see how you greet the day?
Leaving the house in slippers?
Opening wider as if you could bear more?

Keepsake

Haines Sprunt Tate

In her breast they found a density.
Sounds they made against her body,
even sounds she could not hear,
would not go through it.

She would place one finger there
or there — her wishing would dissolve it.
It would melt away with the many months,
the many months of snow, it would melt away.

It was oh nothing, air,
or a piece of her that escaped loving,
a story she'd told no one, a fluid tale
hardened like a stone under her skin.

They told her no harm, no harm,
it was not what she could fear.
This ache was rootless, self-contained.
They said she would feel nothing

but their touch, she would not sleep
and when they opened her she would be
there and nowhere, and after it remember
nothing. For all their work they said

she'd keep one thin, thin scar.

One of the Dummies at Night

Gibson Fay-LeBlanc

He slept in the tinder box
his master made, and oak
grain governed the dreaming —

his left eye clouded over,
he closed the other and saw
mild applause in his future.

His bed sat at a crevice
edge, pure pitch below,
and a cold wind slowed

the senses, rising from who
knows where. Later his mind
became its pin, eschewed

dowels and string and leapt
into the dark. The fall
was pleasurable, apt:

there were no voices
in the breeze, no speeches
to open his mouth.

Snow

Elizabeth Tibbetts

The old, blue-eyed woman in the bed
is calling down snow. Her heart is failing,
and her eyes are two birds in a pale sky.
Through the window she can see a tree

twinkling with lights on the banking
beyond the parking lot. Lawns are still green
from unseasonable weather. Snow
will put things right; and sure enough,

by four, darkness carries in the first flakes.
Chatter, hall lights, and the rattle of walkers
spill through her doorway as she lies there —
ten miles (half a world) of ocean

between her and her home island.
She looks out from a bed the size of a dinghy.
Beyond the lit tree, beyond town, open water
accepts snow silently and, farther out,

the woods behind her house receive the snow
with a faint ticking of flakes striking needles
and dry leaves—a sound you would not believe
unless you've held your breath and heard it.

Another Full Moon

Kate Barnes

The house, lit by moonlight
on the snow, glows inside
like a huge jewel, a moonstone
or opal.
  The whole house
shimmers with its freight
of living souls, and the souls
of disembodied memory.
                          I lie
inside my warm bed in the cold
brightness, dreaming of those
who can no longer dream
of anyone, who have become
motes of dust
in the air, those universal
dreamers.
    You would imagine,
looking into the next room,
that a lamp was lit,
but I know it is only
the light of the moon
westering, nearly full,
over the snow.

I am not wanting
or asking anything
impossible; it's just
that I can't help
thinking about it.

Prayer for Joy

Stuart Kestenbaum

What was it we wanted
to say anyhow, like today
when there were all the letters
in my alphabet soup and suddenly
the 'j' rises to the surface.
The 'j', a letter that might be
great for scrabble, but not really
used for much else, unless
we need to jump for joy,
and then all of a sudden
it's there and ready to
help us soar and to open up
our hearts at the same time,
this simple line with a curved bottom,
an upside down cane that helps
us walk in a new way into this
forest of language, where all the letters
are beginning to speak,
finding each other in just
the right combination
to be understood.

El Café a la Esquina de Agua y Vida, Seville

Jeffrey Thomson

Near the café at the corner of Water and Life
in the plaza of blood oranges at the bend
of the whitewash and archways of old stone,
between the congregation of traffic and
the soft hammers of the cathedral bells,
near baths made by Peter the Cruel and
alongside the tiny carapaces of smartcars
hived in the old Jewish quarter where
the exhausted-piss-whiff of the city
wanders off into the Jardines de Murillo
where fists of palms and geometric rigmarole
circle the fountain — ficus and terra cotta
frescoes of the Christian everlasting:
the gold leaf, the halo, Madonna adoring —
near the dead-end of the road of death,
beneath keyhole arches at the mark of midyear
and in the shadow of el Real Alcázar (layered
cathedral of all that's holy here — Christian
on Muslim on Roman on something far older),
where wings of the canopy angle out to hide me
from the wallop of the noonday sun in the square
where I'm sipping a vinho verde that tastes
like the effervescence of granite and hot straw,
the woman at the public fountain, with an ache

and a fine delicacy, runs damp hands through
her spray of dark hair, sops the hot arch
of her neck, and trails fingers down her bare
arms the way Christ might have washed Magdelane
had he been a just bit more human.

At the Metropolitan Museum of Art

Eve Forti

Transitory impressions: shiny
face in silver compact mirror,
tongue on teeth, lips curled.
She seems unaware
as Degas winks somewhere.
What would Renoir say?
Or Monet?
It appears she doesn't care.

She could be posing in a ladies lounge
or subway station.
Her rapt glance drawn to herself,
her admiring eyes
focused on her admiring eyes
and freshly painted mouth.
No broken color there.
But the luminosity, the brilliance.
A masterpiece of sorts.

Shell

Annie Finch

and then I felt a yearning
to stare out at the sea —
or simply at the stretching sand —
the waters restlessly

beating with their own chaos in,
as fall's late wind blew cold
and spoke in whispers at my earth
at I was growing old —

days were growing shorter,
I was growing too,
and soon there would be nothing more
than words that I might rue.

And then I went and folded in
upon myself, and found
in my dark folds a small white shell,
and put it on the ground.

Her Harvest

Thomas Carper

She stitched her life together. Folded leaves
Of manuscript, gathered and bound with thread,
Become the harvest of her days, the sheaves
That would survive long after she was dead.
We turn the pages, following where her hand
Recorded, as though glintings on a brook,
The bursts of thought that seem still to command
Untold attentions everywhere we look.
And yet we feel we never quite arrive
At the illuminations she achieved;
Her restless poems are ever more alive
As further revelations are received
When we seek for new meaning in what lies
Beneath the words that pass before our eyes.

First Fig and Second Fig

Edna St. Vincent Millay

My candle burns at both ends;
    It will not last the night;
But, ah, my foes, and oh, my friends —
    It gives a lovely light!

. . . . .

Safe upon the solid rock the ugly houses stand:
Come and see my shining palace built upon the sand.

8

What Happened Back Then

Mother Tongue

Mihku Paul

Stolen child, stranger with no name.
Her mouth has been sewn shut.
The songs, on their long flight,
years upon years, birth upon death, lost.
Mute witness, what silence is this?
Unfortunate demise, flesh and bone,
language we lived by,
scattered like pollen dust,
the trace of finest powder.
Possessed, our teeth clack and grind,
purpled lips slap and curl, a strangled wailing:
tuberculosis, dysentery, pneumonia.
One thousand ways to kill a thing, and
only one true way to save it:
Our words, shape of sounds no longer familiar,
buried at Carlisle.
Oh, Grandmother, we are wandering now.
The map obscured, ripped and bloodied.
We speak a strange tongue.
    We are ghosts, haunting ourselves.

Sardine Packer

Tom Sexton

The moon drew the bay to itself
like a lover at full tide
when I was young and full of life.
Oh, I could make my scissors dance.

Silver fish spilled from every net,
and all my days were buttery
when I worked at the cannery.
Oh, I could make my scissors dance.

My children came to see me work.
I was the fastest on the line.
They liked to slide in herring slime.
Oh, I could make my scissors dance.

The new owner won't come to town
to watch us nip and cut and pack.
He bought and gave us all the sack.
Oh, I could make my scissors dance.

My daughter's made her final bow.
My grandson's crying on my knee.
But they can't live on scenery.
Oh, I could make my scissors dance.

Summer people come here now
to walk along the quiet bay.
I had my time. I had my day.
Oh, I could make my scissors dance.

The Mill

Edwin Arlington Robinson

The miller's wife had waited long,
  The tea was cold, the fire was dead;
And there might yet be nothing wrong
  In how he went and what he said:
"There are no millers any more,"
  Was all that she had heard him say;
And he had lingered at the door
  So long that it seemed yesterday.

Sick with a fear that had no form,
  She knew that she was there at last;
And in the mill there was a warm
  And mealy fragrance of the past.
What else there was would only seem
  To say again what he had meant;
And what was hanging from a beam
  Would not have heeded where she went.

And if she thought it followed her,
  She may have reasoned in the dark
That one way of the few there were
  Would hide her and would leave no mark:
Black water, smooth above the weir
  Like starry velvet in the night,
Though ruffled once, would soon appear
  The same as ever to the sight.

The House on the Hill

Edwin Arlington Robinson

They are all gone away,
    The House is shut and still,
There is nothing more to say.

Through broken walls and gray
    The winds blow bleak and shrill:
They are all gone away.

Nor is there one today
    To speak them good or ill:
There is nothing more to say.

Why is it then we stray
    Around the sunken sill?
They are all gone away,

And our poor fancy-play
    For them is wasted skill:
There is nothing more to say.

There is ruin and decay
In the House on the Hill:
They are all gone away,
There is nothing more to say.

The Old Gross Place

Patricia Ranzoni

Across the road the
    old dairy is an apparition.
Not haunted so much as
    that it is, itself, a ghost.
When I go for mail, Hazel
    is not in the kitchen.
Mary is not upstairs, Tom
    not in his chair
by the window. White sheers
    are an absence I promise
to remember.
    One could watch forever
and never see them again.
    Search clean through
those waving old panes
    front to back, not a soul
not even a stick of their furniture
    to rest wavy eyes
on. Why, a neighbor
    can look clear through
that thinning house
    all the way to heaven.

The Granite Stoop

Tom Sexton

I walked past it from time to time
in a wood that had once been cleared
for a family farm before the Revolution.
Oxen hauled it inland from the coast.
A still visible depression in the earth
marked where a house once stood.
There was a clear spring not far away
and the worn slates of a burial ground.

I remember that the stoop was as tall
as a two year old. How many generations
coming and going at dawn and dusk
wore the ladle-shaped groove in its center
that spilled heavy rain from its lip
and held the icy stars when it was cold?

Recuerdo

Edna St. Vincent Millay

We were very tired, we were very merry —
We had gone back and forth all night on the ferry.
It was bare and bright, and smelled like a stable —
But we looked into a fire, we leaned across a table,
We lay on a hill-top underneath the moon;
And the whistles kept blowing, and the dawn came soon.

We were very tired, we were very merry —
We had gone back and forth all night on the ferry;
And you ate an apple, and I ate a pear,
From a dozen of each we had bought somewhere;
And the sky went wan, and the wind came cold,
And the sun rose dripping, a bucketful of gold.

We were very tired, we were very merry —
We had gone back and forth all night on the ferry.
We hailed, "Good morrow, mother!" to a shawl-covered head,
And bought a morning paper, which neither of us read;
And she wept, "God bless you!" for the apples and pears,
And we gave her all our money but our subway fares.

October Moon

Claire Hersom

I see you every so often;
at the grade school parking lot,
the House of Pizza,
driving down by the lake near the Legion.

You have a painter cap on,
your expression a half smile,
and if I close my eyes, I can
feel your mouth kissing mine
under the October moon,
the mill stream steady beside us,
me, hungry to pour life back into
a splintered heart.

Under red and gold branches,
windows of the town dark,
we held hands, hip to hip, and kissed
until the world lost its balance.
Twenty years later, you pass me in a car,
your wife and your daughter talking,
moving a hand, brushing hair from a brow
or reaching forward. One hand on the wheel
lifts a hello in my direction.
We smile.

The Lost Seed

Edward J. Reilly

Burying my dog was easier than plowing
a field, harder than planting an Easter bulb
for spring blooming. We expected no great crop
from this digging, this planting the seed
of childhood, barks frozen in the slightly open mouth,
the feet that ran to call now slower than molasses,
warm petting-flesh flat and hard, life to leather.

I dreamed, though, there might be some bloom,
yellow or purple, leaning its fragile head into sun,
a thin, green-leaved stalk with a touch of perfume.
I watched, instead, the summer come and go, winter
fall white and cold, other seasons, an eternity
or two: and the hard silence unbearable at times —
a hand aching to be licked, fingers stroking air.

When I Was a Little Cuban Boy

Richard Blanco

O José can you see . . . that's how I sang it, when I was
a cubanito in Miami, and América was some country
in the glossy pages of my history book, someplace
way north, everyone white, cold, perfect. This Land
is my Land, so why didn't I live there, in a brick house
with a fireplace, a chimney with curlicues of smoke.
I wanted to wear breeches and stockings to my chins,
those black pilgrim shoes with shiny gold buckles.
I wanted to eat yams with the Indians, shake hands
with los negros, and dash through snow I'd never seen
in a one-horse hope-n-say? I wanted to speak in British,
say really smart stuff like fours core and seven years ago
or one country under God, in the visible. I wanted to see
that land with no palm trees, only the strange sounds
of flowers like petunias, peonies, impatience, waiting
to walk through a door someday, somewhere in God
Bless America and say, Lucy, I'm home, honey. I'm home.

Laughter

Stuart Kestenbaum

You know the kind of laughter
when you laugh so hard and unexpectedly
you can snort liquid right through
your nose, like the soda you were drinking.
That's what happened to me with a milkshake
when I was 11 years old and too worried
for my own good. My uncle and I were swapping
book jokes. "Have you read Tiger's Revenge
by Claude Balls?" he asks, which strikes me
as so funny that I begin to laugh
uncontrollably and milk is dripping from my nose
almost like I've thrown up, but instead
I feel incredibly light and happy.
That's the kind of laughter that even
if you have been crying and heard someone
else laughing, you would start to laugh.
It spreads like a wind passing
through leaves, it makes the bitter muscle
of the heart unclench itself. Imagine,
all this from only eight words from my uncle,
and one of those a preposition
with only two letters.

Hunger for Something Easier

Rachel Contreni Flynn

I suppose now you'll deny it all:
there was no wild pig in the woods,
hair up on his back like barbed wire,
eyes sunk and runny in crusted tunnels
along the snout. And we didn't run
through red brambles, banging our legs
against stumps until we flung ourselves
into the thorny arms of an apple tree.
You'll say we didn't stay shoved up
against the bark breathing bright spice
and pitching green fruit to frighten away
the pig. You'll never say you were afraid
or that I held you and you held me
and we crouched on the thin branches
until night slunk in, and a hunger
for something easier turned the pig away.

Homering Among the Pines

Edward J. Reilly

With my old, pockmarked bat,
but without a ball, I played
the game as perfectly as any
summer hero. I used, instead,

the pine cones that dropped
at random from the pines overhead
littering the lawn, shooting out
of the lawnmower against my legs

as I mowed, but ready to fill
the air with home runs when I
turned to sport. The small dry cones
whizzed like insects at the moment

I stroked them, fluttering like
butterflies when their velocity
suddenly declined. Oh, how I hit
those brown cones, and sometimes,

lining one just right with my bat
between layers of wind, I sent it
high up through dark branches,
returning to whence it came, and all

the invisible baseball spirits
on all my invisible bases raced
for home as I dropped my bat
and waved to the surrounding wind.

The School Bus

Christian Barter

In the dream I was getting on the school bus
from the back of the bus for some reason, only this time
instead of jeers and everyone sliding over
to the aisle-side so I couldn't sit down, someone said,
"There's a seat up here, Chris." It was

next to Mary Jo Stillwell, pretty as she was
in eighth grade, who had slid to the window
to let me sit, and when a kid put me in a headlock
I simply lifted him over my head and set him
in the seat in front of me, said, "Stay there,"

and a little boy had grabbed a little girl
by the hair, only this time I pulled him off
and sat him down, saying, "You don't ever grab a girl,"
and sat her down, too, and asked her if she was all right.
No one jeered at this, or swore at me,

or threatened my life for disrupting the ways things
were supposed to be on the school bus going to
Mountain View Middle School in Sullivan, Maine —
if that's even where we were going —
and when I sat back in my seat, Mary Jo leaned forward

in a very serious manner, and I kissed her
as though it were the most natural thing to do
with Mary Jo — short, serious kisses — on that
school bus that was nothing like any school bus I had ever ridden,
that was exactly like every school bus I have ever ridden,
and when she started kissing my neck in a way that tickled,
I woke up exactly in my life.

Geography

Marcia F. Brown

In eighth grade, Matilda
Savino held us in her thrall
by dangling
for 50 minutes of Geography
one loafer precariously
from her toe.

Right knee crossed over her left.
tiny skirt high on her thighs,
she let the well-worn loafer loll
back and forth, back
and forth, clinging
against physics
to her otherwise bare
and shapely foot.

Mr. Perkins couldn't keep his eyes off it
and forgot the names of continents,
while we all sat
in shocked, delicious anticipation—
waiting to record the seismic shift
of one shoe dropping,
then the other.

The Light

Stuart Kestenbaum

A Camel-smoking teenager, I have just returned
from New York City with my friend
Ellen, she of the wispy blonde
hair in her eyes and the sophisticated
laugh, when a moth dives deep
into my throat, so that I can't
talk or swallow. We are on the way
to her house for what I pray will be
love, and I can't even tell her
what has happened, I just
stand there in the mercury vapor
light on South Orange Avenue
until we part and I walk home.
The day in New York with the visits
to her genteel friends,
the Metropolitan Museum of Art,
and Art Students League and the
exotic promise of the train station
all behind us, I knew I just wanted
a girl to put in my life to make
me whole and instead I swallow
a moth, the brown and white
moth that circles endlessly around
the glow, that can burn itself on the
candle of desire. It must have been

after the light that was
inside me, the light that
even after all these years
I have not yet seen or understood.

Gold Stars

Rachel Contreni Flynn

It was forbidden to touch
the Hummels in my aunt's pretty house,
arranged just so and shut
in the glass cabinet, pigeon-toed,
rosy-faced, holding kittens or balloons,
their porcelain bellies bulging
under pinafores and overalls . . .

and it was wrong to kiss
the high-school janitor after track practice
against the concrete wall
in the band room vestibule
where a fake velvet blanket draped
the old upright piano,
and a long row of trombones tilted
in their shiny black cases . . .

but these
were the gold stars I gave myself
when I thought no one was watching
and nothing would get broken,
and I was brilliant: easing

the little brass latches
and reaching in.

Salt and Pepper

Sheila Gray Jordan

After grace, his next words
would be, "Pass
the salt and pepper,"
never the one without the other,
though a guest at his table,
a stranger to this courtesy, might ask
for salt or pepper.
And we would pass them both.
The Morton Salt walked
its girl with her umbrella
through the rain in the kitchen,
under her arm a box
pouring salt: when it rains
it pours — a negligence
or lesson, I could not be sure.
Mother measured a pinch
in the palm of her hand.
Still he lifted the wide-holed shaker,
salting the salty dinner,
not adding pepper. "Unhealthy,"
she warned.
At the funeral, she places a rose.
We cup our handfuls of dirt.
It falls on his coffin
like too much pepper.

A Notable Failure

Robert Siegel

He never went abroad to broaden him,
and though he learned to read, he did not write
anything worth saving. Once, at a whim,
he scribbled something they hadn't gotten right

in the sand and erased it. Few could know
whether to credit any of the vulgar rumors
surrounding his birth in a shed. There were low
whispers and a gap of thirty years.

Then more rumors trickled through the countryside
about the artisan's son turned wonderworker:
probably a charlatan — blasphemer to be sure. Wide-eyed,
some claimed he raised the dead (and healed lepers!)
before the Romans nailed him — as they nailed all such —
and the neighbors sniffed, "He didn't come to much!"

The Silent Seers

J. Barrie Shepherd

Of all the witnesses
around that holy manger
perhaps it was the animals
who saw best what lay ahead,
for they had paced the aching roads
slept in the wet and hungry fields,
known the sharp sting of sticks
and thorns and curses,
and endured the constant bruise
of burdens not their own,
given the tendency of men
to use and then discard
rather than meet and pay
the debt of gratitude.
For them the future also held
the knacker's rope, the flayer's blade,
the tearing of their bodies
for the sparing of a race.
In the shadows of that stable
might it be his warmest welcome
lay within their quiet comprehending gaze?

The Meeting

Henry Wadsworth Longfellow

After so long an absence
  At last we meet again:
Does the meeting give us pleasure,
  Or does it give us pain?

The tree of life has been shaken,
  And but few of us linger now,
Like the Prophet's two or three berries
  In the top of the uppermost bough.

We cordially greet each other
  In the old, familiar tone;
And we think, though we do not say it,
  How old and gray he is grown!

We speak of a Merry Christmas
  And many a Happy New Year;
But each in his heart is thinking
  Of those that are not here.

We speak of friends and their fortunes,
  And when they did and said,
Till the dead alone seem living,
  And the living alone seem dead.

And at last we hardly distinguish
    Between the ghosts and the guests;
And a mist and shadow of sadness
    Steals over our merriest jests.

Old Whitman Loved Baseball

Edward J. Reilly

Old Whitman loved baseball, covered it
for Brooklyn newspapers, watched games
every chance he got, talked about it
endlessly to anyone who would listen
when he grew too old and ill to get about.
He never got over, though, the new curveball
and the deceit that went with it. Thought
it un-American, not the stuff of noble youth
or democracy. He must have seen what was coming.

Faith

Robert M. Chute

I've never found an arrowhead,
one flinty chip of history.
Young Thoreau, they said, if he walked by
some farmer's fresh-plowed field, could just
stoop down and pick one up. As if
the spirit that had shaped them drew them
up to his attention. Stoney bread crumbs
no birds will eat, these points and flakes
led him from the town into the
saving woods and wilderness, marked
the path to a wildness which might
save us all. It was his faith
that led him. We find, he said,
what we are prepared to see.

9

Together and Apart

Thicker Than Country

Richard Blanco

A Cuban like me living in Maine? Well,
what the hell, Mark loves his native snow
and I don't mind it, really. I love icicles,
even though I still decorate the house
with seashells and starfish. Sometimes
I want to raise chickens and pigs, wonder
if I could grow even a small mango tree
in my three-season porch. But mostly,
I'm happy with hemlocks and birches
towering over the house, their shadows
like sundials, the cool breeze blowing
even in the summer. Sometimes I miss
the melody of Spanish, a little, and I play
Celia Cruz, dance alone in the basement.
Sometimes I miss the taste of white rice
with picadillo — so I cook, but it's never
as good as my mother's. I don't miss her
or the smell of her Cuban bread as much
as I should. Most days I wonder why, but
when Mark comes home like an astronaut
dressed in his ski clothes, or I spy him
planting petunias in the spring, his face
smudged with this earth, or barbequing
in the summer when he asks me if I want
a hamberg or a cheezberg as he calls them —

still making me laugh after twelve years —
I understand why the mountains here
are enough, white with snow or green
with palms, mountains are mountains,
but love is thicker than any country.

Valentine

Linda Aldrich

–for David

In that fragile turn of time just out of sleep
before memory of what this year has been,
you bring wood to start the fire. It snowed again.
To grind coffee quietly is impossible, but you keep
the radio volume low. I don't know when you first
brought me coffee in bed. My mother died
six months ago. I was preoccupied
and didn't notice the first warm cup, though
once I heard you whisper the dog back into bed
so I could feel the comfort of his head against my feet.
Loss begets loss (or so I've heard it said),
but there's finding, too, and the heart's repletion,
so put the cup down on the table, love.
Let the body of our sonnet find completion.

Why I Have A Crush On You, UPS Man

Alice N. Persons

you bring me all the things I order
are never in a bad mood
always have a jaunty wave as you drive away
look good in your brown shorts
we have an ideal uncomplicated relationship
you're like a cute boyfriend with great legs
who always brings the perfect present
(why, it's just what I've always wanted!)
and then is considerate enough to go away
oh, UPS Man, let's hop in your clean brown truck and elope!
ditch your job, I'll ditch mine
let's hit the road for Brownsville
and tempt each other
with all the luscious brown foods —
roast beef, dark chocolate,
brownies, Guinness, homemade pumpernickel, molasses cookies
I'll make you my mama's bourbon pecan pie
we'll give all the packages to kind-looking strangers
live in a cozy wood cabin
with a brown dog or two
and a black and brown tabby
I'm serious, UPS Man. Let's do it.
Where do I sign?

The Lady and the Tramp

Bruce Guernsey

As my mother's memory dims,
she's losing her sense of smell
and can't remember the toast
blackening the kitchen with smoke
or sniff how nasty the breath of the dog
that follows her yet from room to room,
unable, himself, to hear his own bark.

It's thus they get around,
the wheezing old hound stone deaf
baying like a smoke alarm
for his amnesiac mistress, whose back
from petting him is bent forever
as they shuffle towards the flaming toaster
and split the cindered crisp that's left.

Briefly, Enough

Candice Stover

this morning light trembled
through my lashes
as I drifted in and out
of sleep, cheek resting
on my love's chest

I could follow every breath

a breeze passing over our bodies moved
like another breath, another
kind of breathing, until it seemed
we were drowsing on an open vessel
on a body of water we did not need to name

Summer

Jacob Fricke

for Jennifer Hickey

I touched the face of midnight once
though it was scarcely noon —
the breezes ghost-like in the grass
presented their perfume.

I fell on fields beneath the sky
and summer was my bed,
the heat and shade for counterpane,
the ground to cup my head.

Then — sweet, sweet, sweet my falling lid —
the skies began to close,
and blank before my sluggish eyes,
a world for my repose.

Young Pine

Carl Little

The white pine that happened to grown
eedles-to-clapboard at the back of the shed
looks as if it is hiding

from the cops or a gang,
or is simply playing hide-and-seek,
a nine-year-old girl, say,

with gentle boughs
hugging the corner of the outbuilding,
trembling in a breeze, hoping

no one notices her until
she can reach a size where the house owner
won't consider her

spindly enough to be cut down.
Lithe, small, hidden,
the young pine is beautiful.

Someone should embrace her
as she grows toward the roof line,
save her from the saw.

Freeze Frame

Marcia F. Brown

Camera, tripod, satchel of gear
shouldered under dry branches,
you are headed out to take a picture
of the loon we think
will winter over on the salt pond.

In the upstairs window, pen in hand,
I am framing this picture of you
intent on your mission: green shirt,
gray vest in the mottled light
of Indian summer.

Beloved, you walk as much with this world
as the deer. How do I say
how the hay-gold grasses
bend to you? How the split rails
draw you to their vanishing point,

beyond which, a bird   wild
and ancient, sends up
its hollow, fluted cry
and how for one moment, I long
to know a distant song,

something I can sing
to hold you there.

Burning in the Rain

Richard Blanco

Someday compassion would demand
I set myself free of my desire to recreate
my father, indulge in my mother's losses,
strangle lovers with words, forcing them
to confess for me and take the blame.
Today was that day: I tossed them, sheet
by sheet on the patio and gathered them
into a pyre. I wanted to let them go
in a blaze, tiny white dwarfs imploding
beside the azaleas and ficus bushes,
let them crackle, burst like winged seeds,
let them smolder into gossamer embers —
a thousand gray butterflies in the wind.
Today was that day, but it rained, kept
raining. Instead of fire, water — drops
knocking on doors, wetting windows
into mirrors reflecting me in the oaks.
The garden walls and stones swelling
into ghostlier shades of themselves,
the wind chimes giggling in the storm,
a coffee cup left overflowing with rain.
Instead of burning, my pages turned
into water lilies floating over puddles,
then tiny white cliffs as the sun set,
finally drying all night under the moon
into papier-mâché souvenirs. Today
the rain would not let their lives burn.

After Twenty Years

Dawn Potter

It is possible
that no husband really loves his wife.

Too easy it is to mistake
their scheduled arrivals and departures, their constancy,
for something greater than the dim outcroppings
of loneliness.

When, entrapped again
in the fervent throes of habit,
we cry, "Do you love me?"
they answer yes.

Their manners
are faultless, restrained.
They sleep deeply,
and, in the morning, scraping ashes from the stove,

only rarely do they forget to speak.

The Man in Front of You

Alice N. Persons

is just tall enough
has soft black hair
and golden skin
wide shoulders
and smells good

you stand behind him
in the movie line
or buying flowers on boylston street
or see him on the subway
not far down the car
his clean brown hands
on the overhead rail

the man in front of you
could have just killed someone
or might have a bitter face
may love no one
or always sleep alone

the man in front of you
hurries out of the station
or rushes around the corner
and vanishes into a cab
you never see his face
but in dreams he comes to you
and does not slip away

Balloon

Haines Sprunt Tate

for D.

This is the poem I meant to give you
for your birthday: a kind of balloon
that would rise on a slight draft
to float above the occasion,
taut and bright and full of easy breath
with a long ribbon trailing down
for holding onto or tying to your chair.
After you'd opened all the presents
while everyone oohed and ahhed,
after the cake and candles,
the joker gifts and For He's a Jolly
Good Fellow and they'd all gone home
glad it hadn't been their turn
to blow the flame off another year,
that's when I meant to say, Look,
Love, what I made for you:
Take it and don't let go —

But now your birthday's done
and I'd be heartless to remind you
with a thing deflated, wrinkling,
that bumps the corners of the hall
more off-kilter every day,
so far from its highest aspirations.

Though I almost think you'd crack
a smile to see how it's outlasted
all the fuss: the cake, the cards
and all the company but one
old procrastinator, old hanger-on.

Closure

Weslea Sidon

Two years after he died
she came back to the field
they had last walked as lovers.

For decades
touch had been their sport and refuge —
hands, lips always finding new delights
in old passion.

She could sense him now,
his steady arm holding her
the first time she raised
her timid lips to his,
the last time as she raised her eager mouth
to shush the laughter above his silver beard.

She could sense him too soon after,
the illness souring his lips,
his fingers pushing hers away,
closing each button she opened,
refusing even memory of ecstasy.

She came back to the field to see
if the stand of lupine
had held the shape of her memories
long enough to give them back,

if love left a trail
that she could follow forward
even as it closed behind.

The Solemn Son

Thomas Carper

"It's his." They'll weigh it out behind the store.
Harry Nason writes the boy's name, Steve
Burnell. The boy looks solemnly at the floor,
Trying to work it out. It's hard to believe
That in one deafening moment in the woods,
At daybreak, as he shivered from the cold,
So much could change. He overhears his dad's
Words as Harry has the story told.
"Two shots . . . the heart." He'd hardly time to see
The buck before the crashing blasts that killed
Him rang in his ears so overpoweringly
That just when he was sure he'd be fulfilled
He felt dazed and deserted. Now the son
Hears Harry's voice from miles away. "Well done."

My Mother's Funeral

Ira Sadoff

The Rabbi doesn't say she was sly and peevish,
fragile and voracious, disheveled, voiceless and useless,
at the end of her very long rope. He never sat beside her
like a statue while radio voices called to her from God.
He doesn't say how she mamboed with her broom,
staggered, swayed, and sighed afternoons,
till we came from school to feel her. She never frightened him,
or bent to kiss him, sponged him with a fever, never held his hand,
bone-white, bolted doors, and shut the blinds. She never sent
roaches in a letter, he never saw her fall down stairs, dead sober.
He never watched her sweep and murmur, he never saw
spiderwebs she read as signs her life was over, long before
her frightened husband left, long before
they dropped her in a box, before her children turned
shyly from each other, since they never learned to pray.
If I must think of her, if I can spare her moment on the earth,
I'll say she was one of God's small sculptures,
polished to a glaze, one the wind blew off a shelf.

The Pain Sweepstakes

Mekeel McBride

is open to all, regardless of age,
opportunity, or interest. Takes no
effort to enroll. When you win, you
win big and we aren't just bragging. Imagine
your cat, flat as a cartoon in the aftermath
of a foreign car; discover your favorite
child feeding on the fine caviar
of barbiturates; find your spouse in bed
with a young student of Russian literature
whose pink cheeks shine like the Ukranian
dawn. If all else fails we can crack your father's
heart like a walnut left over from last
Christmas, then hook him up to the white heaven
of intensive care. We care about you.
For once, we want you to win.
And the really startling part is how easy
this all is. Keep your hopes high. We draw
your number every time you sigh at the sad
shape this world is in.

The Present

Bruce Guernsey

For her birthday that year
I bought my mother
one of those portable phones,
the new kind you could carry
all over the house
so she wouldn't be alone
anywhere anymore,

except she couldn't remember
where she'd left it
most of the time those days
and hurried in her slippers
from one room to the next
only to hear it ringing
somewhere down the hall

and opened the front door
to no one there
or still on the phone
when she finally found it
where she never put it,
the house getting bigger
as she got smaller

but no less busy
than she was before
with us six kids
and my father at work, or war —
that new phone like having us
still around, calling from somewhere,
upstairs or down.

Fog-Talk

Philip Booth

Walking the heaved cement sidewalk down Main Street,
I end up where the town bottoms out: a parking lot
thick with sea-fog. There's Wister, my boyhood friend,

parked on the passenger side of his old Dodge pick-up.
He's waiting for Lucia, the girl who drives him around
and feeds him, the one who takes care of him at home.

Wister got married late. Wifeless now, no kids, he's near
sixty-eight. Like me. Watching the ebb, looking out into
the fog. Fog so thick that if you got shingling your roof

you'd shingle three or four courses out onto
the fog before you fell off or sun came. Wister knows
that old joke. Not much else, not any more. His mind drifts

every whichway. When I start over to his old pick-up,
he waves to my wave coming toward him, his window half up,
half down. He forgets how to work it. I put my head

up close. Wister, I say, you got your compass with you
to steer her home through the fog? Wister smiles at me with
all sorts of joy, nodding yes. He says I don't know.

The Man Who Looked Like Elvis

Elizabeth Garber

No one remembers when the man with the pomade-combed
crescendo of jet black hair first appeared,
but we all quietly pay attention to him. Two summers
ago a guitar was strapped over his back when we eyed
him wandering miles along Route 1. Last year, when
his hair was bleached reddish blond, we wondered to
ourselves if he'd given up on Elvis. This spring, his hair
is black again. All over town, we nod the same nod:
Elvis is back. Passing him on High Street we notice
his carefully shaved long sideburns, before our gaze
shifts to the nearby shop windows. He leaves
the supermarket as we arrive. A strange discomfort twists
our faces away. Opening night of Hairspray, in the art
deco neon glow of the movie theater, the crowd is thick
with bleached-blond beehive contestants, sculpted hair
rising like curvaceous mounds of soft ice cream. Elvis
appears with his blunt, heavy brows, the rough-carved
mouth, the deep-plowed wrinkles under his eternal
pompadour. In the competition for the biggest, tallest
hair, we cheer for rhinestone glasses, pedal pushers,
bobby socks. Later, when we chat and smile, trying
to hide the hunger of our loneliness, he slips
through the forest of lacquered hair, a silent king
passing among us, searching for his subjects, his
promised land, a place where he, too, will be recognized.

Exit

Edwin Arlington Robinson

For what we owe to other days,
Before we poisoned him with praise,
May we who shrank to find him weak
Remember that he cannot speak.

For envy that we may recall,
And for our faith before the fall,
May we who are alive be slow
To tell what we shall never know.

For penance he would not confess,
And for the fateful emptiness
Of early triumph undermined,
May we now venture to be kind.

Elegy for the Stepfather

Bruce Willard

Only a month ago I imagined sailing with him
on the ketch he built. His oversized hands
on the tiller. Sails fathered by a sou'west breeze.

He, who came like a front into my home
and stole my wind a decade ago.
Who gave it back in the way he tendered my son.
Trimmed the parts that were neither his nor mine
alone to love.

This strange, familial wind we rode and shared,
separated us, paired us on tack,
only to separate us again.

Becalmed, I miss him now,
just the small boat of his ashes left.
These storms which have no names,
the ghostly calm
which leaves no wake.

A Prayer, A Welcome

David Walker

Little wrinkle
from my flesh, eyelid

curling down at my fool's
prattle; child

before whom I'm the more
child — your future

older than my past…
Forgive the father

I'll be, become all
I can never know;

teach me to hold
you for a while, and then

to let go.

After Another Difficult Week

Linda Aldrich

In French, pendant means hanging, like pomegranates,
like persimmons, like ideas you keep afloat for poems
that finally find their way to you. Like friends
waning to slivers of moon, then rounding
like the world again, dropping gifts in your lap.
This morning, a pair of bees in my mailbox —
a gold bee pendant from Crete — where she found it
in an alley shop. Two bees holding a drop of honey
between them, an amber bead kept from falling.
Outside my window, the second foot of snow is coming down.
I watched rhododendrons become mounds of white
sadness, like hasty graves. But now this.
How unexpected is summer's sudden memory.
How easily it buzzes and brims over the morning.

Valentines

Marcia F. Brown

Flame in the snow-bowed lilac tree,
flare of yellow beak, coal nugget eye —
I want to call you jubilantly
and I do — Come, quickly — Look!
And you do, and there we are
at the kitchen window, my hands
damp above the suds, you
in your storm coat, halfway out the door
to shovel a foot of new snow. Both of us
suddenly blissful and buoyed
by this eruption of red
in the flocked and frosted
wedding cake of our yard. Now
he is joined by the muted rose
of his mate. If they had something to do,
it seems to be right here, poised
between frozen buds, the storm
moving out to sea, an unexpected sunset
lighting the trees like glass, tinting
the long field coral. Startling too,
how together, they unfold like paper hearts
and are gone.

Thousand Dollar Thumbs

Robin Merrill

You cut the left one off with a table saw.
Good doctor sewed it back on. Called you lucky.
Next summer, the right one got gobbled up
by a bear trap. Took twenty stitches to repair it.
Driving home, your father coined the pair:
your thousand dollar thumbs. I didn't know
these stories the first time I felt them,
left one bigger than it should be and crooked.
right one shrunken and hard as a knot,
scarred up like maps my fingers followed.
Ugly and perfect, your thumbs traced out my spine.
Callous caress so extraordinary, call me lucky.
Now our grandkids hang off them, unaware of their history.
Now morning's clumsy thumbs fumble shirt buttons.
But I am here to help you. Call us both lucky.

Chick Magnets

Thomas Moore

It's the Patriots' home opener
and I'm at a poetry opening in Maine.
The Pats are playing the Cincinnati Bengals,
yet Tom Brady is here at the poetry reading!
"Tom," I say, "why aren't you in Foxborough?"

"Oh," he says, "I've always liked poetry
and I'm making seventy-two mil'
so I can do what I want —
Coach Belichick isn't too happy, though."

The poets read about Cranberry Island,
mice in bread boxes, dragon-flies,
Morocco, eating oysters in Grand Central Station,
summer cottages, and, well, you know,
the kind of stuff poets write about:
heartbreak, and a lot of asters by the side of the road.

"This Savory and James is good stuff," says Tom
after the reading. "Smoother than Bud Light,
and being here is a lot easier than throwing passes"

— his left knee twitches and lifts slightly —
"or getting trashed by the Bengals' defense.
Plus, these poetry readings are real chick magnets —
you and I are the only guys here!"

CONTRIBUTORS

Linda Aldrich, from Portland, has published poetry in anthologies, several literary journals, and two collections, *Foothold* and *March and Mad Women*.

Richard Aldridge authored five volumes of poetry and edited three poetry anthologies. He was a secondary school teacher for several years and lived on the Maine coast.

Lynn Ascrizzi of Freedom has published poems in *World Order, Xanadu,* and *Puckerbrush Review.* She was awarded the 1999 Robert Hayden Poetry Fellowship.

Carol Willette Bachofner was the Poet Laureate of Rockland. Her poems have appeared in *Prairie Schooner, The Cream City Review, The Comstock Review,* and *Crab Orchard* Review. She has published four volumes of poetry.

The late **Kate Barnes**, from Union, was the daughter of Maine writers Henry Beston and Elizabeth Coatsworth. The Maine Poet Laureate, she published two full-length collections, *Where the Deer Were* and *Kneeling Orion.*

Christian Barter of Bar Harbor has authored two collections, *In Someone Else's House* and *The Singers I Prefer*. He was a Hodder Fellow at Princeton.

Richard Blanco of Bethel was President Obama's 2013 Inauguration poet. His third collection, *Looking for the Gulf Motel,* won the Paterson Prize.

Louise Bogan, born in Livermore Falls, wrote poetry reviews in the *New Yorker* for many years. Her essential poems appear in *The Blue Estuaries*.

Ted Bookey of Readfield is the author of five books of poems. He is also the editor of the poetry anthology *How Many Cars Have We Been Married?*

The late **Philip Booth**, from Castine, wrote ten books of poetry. His honors include the Poets' Prize and a National Institute of Arts and Letters award.

The late **Henry Braun** wrote several collections of poetry, most recently, *Loyalty: New and Selected Poems*, which won the MWPA poetry award. He lived in Weld.

Sharon Bray of Orland farms family land on the Penobscot River. Her work as a science writer, newspaper journalist, and poet has appeared in various forums, from medical and literary magazines to poetry anthologies.

Bob Brooks has published four chapbooks, and his full-length collection *Unguarded Crossing* was named First Runner-up for the Eric Hoffer Book Award and shortlisted for the Maine Literary Award for poetry. He resides with his wife in Stockton Springs.

Former Poet Laureate of Portland, **Marcia F. Brown** is the author of four collections of poetry, most recently *When We Invented Water*. She lives in Cape Elizabeth.

Linda Buckmaster, former Poet Laureate of Belfast, has published three chapbooks of poetry. Her poems, stories, and essays have been widely published.

Thomas Carper is Professor Emeritus of English at the University of Southern Maine. He has published collections of poetry and is the co-author of the textbook, *Meter and Meaning.*

Robert M. Chute, from Poland Spring, is the author of *Constellations* and many other collections. He won the MWPA Chapbook and Chad Walsh Awards.

Elizabeth Coatsworth lived for many years with her husband, the writer Henry Beston, on a farm in Nobleboro. A versatile author, she published novels, nonfiction, and dozens of children's books, one of which received the Newbery Medal. She also wrote five collections of poetry.

A descendent of the original English settlers of Maine, **Robert P. Tristram Coffin** attended Bowdoin College and later taught there while writing most of his 37 books, which included poetry and history.

Donald Crane lives on the Down East coast above Milbridge. He has had poems published in a number of journals, including the *Café Review*, the *Christian Science Monitor, Passager,* and *Poetry East.*

Marnie Reed Crowell has written books of prose as well as volumes of poetry. She is active with local land trusts and makes her home on Deer Isle.

Jay Davis lives in Portland, where he founded and hosted the Free Street Poetry Slam and The Skinny Second Tuesday Slam. His work has been published in the *Café Review, Monkey's Fist*, and in three chapbooks.

The late **Theodore Enslin**'s early poetry was inspired by Temple, and after he moved to Milbridge in mid-life, he often wrote about the sea. He published numerous books of poetry, notably *Then and Now: New & Selected Poems.*

Annie Farnsworth is an artist, Reiki master, gardener, and poet, who has published both a chapbook and a full-length volume of poetry. She lives in Arundel.

Gibson Fay-LeBlanc of Portland has published his poems widely. His first collection of poems, *Death of a Ventriloquist*, received the Vassar Miller Prize.

Annie Finch of Portland has published over twenty books, including *Spells: New and Selected Poems,* and *A Poet's Craft*, a guide for developing poets.

Marta Rijn Finch divides her time between Vermont and her home on Moosehead Lake. Her books include *A Solitary Piper* and *Complete Poems: A Bilingual Edition,* a translation of the poems of Pernette de Guillet.

Rachel Contreni Flynn's two award-winning collections are *Ice, Mouth, Song*, and *Tongue.* She has received an NEA Fellowship in poetry and lives in Gorham.

Richard Foerster is the author of six poetry collections. He has been honored with two National Endowment for the Arts Fellowships and an Amy Lowell Poetry Traveling Scholarship. He lives in Cape Neddick.

Eve Forti of Bremen won six awards from *Atlanta Review* and first prize in the *Common Ground Review* poetry contest. Her chapbook is *Holding My Breath.*

Jacob Fricke, a former Poet Laureate of Belfast, collaborates with the Jazz group Algorithm. His volume of verse is *This Book of Poems You Found.*

Elizabeth Garber has three collections of poetry, including *True Affections* and *Listening Inside the Dance.* A former Poet Laureate of Belfast, she helped organize the Belfast Poetry Festival.

Gerald George of East Machias has published four books and many articles and poems. His one-act plays have been produced by Acorn Productions and WERU radio.

Kimberly Cloutier Green is the author of *The Next Hunger* and a chapbook, *What Becomes of Words.* She is a recent MacDowell Fellow who lives in Kittery.

Megan Grumbling of Portland has received a Ruth Lilly Fellowship as well as the Vassar Miller Award for her first collection, *Booker's Point.*

Bruce Guernsey, of Bethel, was a Distinguished Professor at Eastern Illinois University. He has published poems in numerous magazines and several books of poetry, including *From Rain.*

A resident of Boothbay, **Ruth F. Guillard** is a musician and teaches the Transcendental Meditation technique. She began writing poetry later in life and recently published the collection, *From Burnham Cove.*

Peter Harris is a Zen priest who lives in Waterville and teaches at Colby College. He is the author of *Blue Hallelujahs*, which won the MWPA chapbook competition, and the collection *Freeing the Hook.*

Nancy Henry, lived in Maine for more than thirty years. An attorney by education, she is the co-founder of Moon Pie Press and has published three full-length collections: *Sarx, Our Lady of Let's All Sing*, and *Who You Are.*

Claire Hersom is the author of *Drowning,* a memoir in poetry and lives in Winthrop. She has received a St. Botolph Emerging Artist grant.

Preston H. Hood served in Vietnam with Seal Team 2 and was for fifteen years a member of Veterans for Peace. He has published two volumes of poetry: *A Chill I Understand* and the chapbook, *The Hallelujah of Listening*, which won the Maine Literary Award for Poetry. He lives in Sanford.

Constance Hunting's collected poems is titled *Natural Things*. She was the founding editor of *Puckerbrush Review* as well as Puckerbrush Press.

Sheila Gray Jordan lives year-round on Chebeague Island. She earned an MFA from the Warren Wilson Program for Writers. At Kenyon College she was an editor for the *Kenyon Review* and directed the Ohio Poetry Circuit. She has published two books of poetry.

Stuart Kestenbaum of Deer Isle has written six collections of poems. The former director of the Haystack School, he was named Poet Laureate of Maine in 2016.

Susan Deborah King is a summer resident of Great Cranberry Island, which often inspires her poems. Her last collection is *Dropping into the Flower.*

Gary Lawless of Nobleboro is co-owner of Gulf of Maine Books, publisher of Blackberry Books, and a widely published poet, with seventeen collections published in the United States and four in Italy.

Carl Little resides in Ellsworth. Winner of the Academy of American Poets Prize, his poems have appeared in several magazines and anthologies, and in *Ocean Drinker: New & Selected Poems.*

Kristen Lindquist lives and works in Camden. She worked many years at the Bread Loaf Writers Conference and has published three collections of poetry, most recently, *Tourists in the Known World.*

Carolyn Locke, a resident of Troy, has done readings in various venues, including WERU radio and the Belfast Poetry Festival, and her work has twice been recognized by the Maine Literary Awards for Poetry.

Henry Wadsworth Longfellow was born in Portland and taught classics at Bowdoin College before joining the faculty at Harvard. A literary celebrity in his day, his narratives such as "The Song of Hiawatha" and "The Courtship of Miles Standish," provided a mythology for a developing America.

The late **Michael Macklin** lived in Portland and Islesboro. He served as a poetry editor for the *Cafe Review,* and on the board of The Maine Writers and Publishers Alliance, publishing his own poems in *Rattle, The Aurorean, Handsome,* and several anthologies.

Bob MacLaughlin lives in Warren. He has been a newspaper sportswriter, magazine editor, and advertising copywriter. His book *Faulty Wiring: The Alzheimer's Poems and Other Memories* was published in 2011 by Moon Pie Press.

Mekeel McBride resides in Kittery, near the Piscataqua River. The author of several collections of poetry, she has received grants from the National Endowment for the Arts and a fellowship from the Bunting Institute.

The late **Elizabeth McFarland** served as poetry editor for the *Ladies Home Journal* from 1948 to 1961, providing six million readers for the work of the eminent American poets of her day. Her own poems, collected in *Over the Summer Water,* appeared posthumously in 2008.

Robin Merrill of Portland is the author of two poetry collections and four children's books. She won a St. Botolph grant for Emerging Artists.

Edna St. Vincent Millay was born in Rockland and raised in Camden, and though she lived in New York City and settled in the Berkshires, she returned to Maine often, featuring it in her more than twenty books of poems. Under eclipse for many years, her verse has been experiencing a much-deserved restoration.

Leslie Moore is a book illustrator from Belfast who has contributed to books for children and adults. Her publications include both poems and essays.

Thomas R. Moore of Belfast has published two collections, *The Bolt-Cutters*, which won a Maine Literary Award for poetry, and *Chet Sawing*.

David Moreau lives in Wayne with his wife and daughter. He has published four books of poetry. David has worked supporting people with developmental disabilities for most of his adult life.

Dave Morrison's poetry has been published in both literary magazines and anthologies. *The Writers Almanac* featured two poems from his book *Clubland,* containing poems written in verse about rock bars. He lives in Camden.

Paul Nelson is a 25-year resident of Machiasport who lives in Hawaii. He is an NEA Fellow and has won an AWP poetry award. Hc has eight collections.

Edward Nobles lives in Bangor. His poems have been published by numerous magazines, including the *Paris Review, Kenyon Review,* and *Gettysburg Review. Library Journal* selected Nobles as one of "24 Poets for the 21st Century."

Mihku Paul's poetry, describing the native experience and the process of acculturation, appears in her collection, *20th Century PowWow Playland.*

Alice N. Persons of Westbrook has published poetry chapbooks and a full-length collection, *Thank Your Lucky Stars*. She runs Maine's Moon Pie Press.

Dawn Potter of Harmony has written three books of poems. Her third, titled *Same Old Story*, was nominated for a *Los Angeles Times* Book Award.

Gary Rainford of Swan's Island, had work in *The Poet's Grin* and served as writer in residence at Acadia National Park. His collection is *Salty Liquor*.

Patricia Smith Ranzoni of Bucksport has published eight collections of poetry, most recently, *Bedding Vows: Love Poems from Outback Maine.*

Edward J. Reilly of Westbrook is a professor of English at Saint Joseph's College. He is the author or editor of approximately two dozen books, including twelve of poetry.

Edwin Arlington Robinson lived much of his life before age thirty in Gardiner, the "Tilbury Town" of his poems. He was a bestselling writer and won the Pulitzer Prize in poetry three times.

Kenneth Rosen lives in Portland. Among his titles are *The Origins of Tragedy, The Hebrew Lion, Reptile Mind,* and *No Snake, No Paradise*. His latest collection is *The Soul, O Ganders, Being Lonely, Flies.*

Ira Sadoff has published eight books of poetry. He is the recipient of NEA and Guggenheim fellowships. His recent collection is *True Faith*.

Marija Sanderling is a librarian who has practiced creative writing since moving to Wells in 1994. Her poems, often concerned with social history and justice, have been published in *Cafe Review* and *Main Street Review.*

A prolific writer of poetry, fiction, and nonfiction, **May Sarton** moved to York in the later part of her career, when she was rediscovered by feminist academics and reviewers, who found themes important to women in both her poetry and her nonfiction and hailed her as an important contemporary American author.

Tom Sexton was Poet Laureate of Alaska, an early editor of *Alaska Quarterly Review*, and founder of the creative writing program at the University of Alaska at Anchorage. Since 2001, he has lived part of the year in Eastport. He has written numerous collections of poetry

J. Barrie Shepherd, who resides on Chebeague Island, has published poetry in several literary magazines as well as his collection, *Between Mirage and Miracle.*

Betsy Sholl of Portland is the author of eight books of poetry, most recently *Otherwise Unseeable*. An NEA fellow, she was Poet Laureate of Maine from 2006 to 2011.

Weslea Sidon lives and writes in West Tremont, Maine. Her debut collection of poetry, published by Red Chain Press, is titled *The Fool Sings.*

The late **Robert Siegel**'s last collection was *Within This Tree of Bones*. He received awards from the NEA, Poetry, and the Ingram Merrill Foundation.

David Sloan of Brunswick has received the Maine Literary Award and the Betsy Sholl Award. His debut collection is *The Irresistible In-Between.*

Pam Burr Smith lives in Brunswick. She has published poetry in many Maine journals, including *Black Fly Review, Cafe Review,* and *Animus*. Her first book of poetry, *Heaven Jumping Woman*, was published in 2011.

Bruce Spang, former Poet Laureate of Portland, teaches English at Scarborough High School. The editor of a recent anthology, *Passion and Pride: Poets In Support of Equality,* and author of two poetry collections, he lives in Falmouth.

Martin Steingesser is a former Poet Laureate of Portland. His poems have been published in *The Sun,* the *New York Times,* and *American Poetry Review*, as well as in his collection *Brothers of Morning*.

Candice Stover's books of poetry include *Poems from the Pond* and *Holding Patterns*, which won the Maine chapbook contest, judged by Mary Oliver.

The late **John Tagliabue**'s first four volumes of poetry preceded two later collections ranging over many years: *The Great Day: Poems, 1962–1983*, and *New and Selected Poems: 1942–1997*. Tagliabue taught poetry and literature at Bates and other schools around the world.

The late **Haines Sprunt Tate** of Waterville published her poems in various literary journals and in her posthumous collection *Strata and Other Poems.*

Ellen M. Taylor's work has appeared in literary journals throughout the United States. She has published two chapbooks of poetry and the full-length collection, *Floating.* Taylor teaches literature and Women's Studies at the University of Maine at Augusta and lives in Appleton.

Jim Glenn Thatcher lives in Yarmouth and teaches at Southern Maine Community College. His poetry has won a number of honors, including five consecutive awards from *New Millennium Writings.*

Jeffrey Thomson, of Farmington, was an NEA Fellow and a Fulbright Scholar. His several poetry collections include *Birdwatching in Wartime*.

Elizabeth Tibbetts, from Hope, has received a Maine Arts Commission Fellowship and a MAC Good Idea Grant. Her book of poems, *In the Well,* won the Bluestem Poetry Award.

Mariana S. Tupper's poetry has appeared in the *Christian Science Monitor, Off the Coast,* and *Maine Times*. She resides in Yarmouth.

Lewis Turco of Dresden Mills is author of fifty-two books, including *The Book of Forms: A Handbook of Poetics,* called "the poets' Bible" since 1968. He has received many awards for his work, including honorary doctorates from The University of Maine at Fort Kent, Ashland University, and Unity College in Maine.

George V. Van Deventer, of Bristol, has served as Executive Director of the Live Poets Society and as editor of *Off the Coast*. In 1997 he developed poetry workshops in elementary schools, reaching more than a thousand students.

The late **David Walker** published his poetry in three collections, including *Moving Out*, which won an Associated Writing Programs Award for poetry.

Bruce Willard, a resident of Boothbay Harbor, has published his poems in several national magazines. His first book of poems is *Holding Ground.*

Sarah Woolf-Wade, a retired teacher and a veteran sailor, lives in New Harbor. Her poems have appeared in many journals, newspapers, and anthologies; and in three collections of poetry, including *Nightsong*.

A former Ruth Lilly poet, **Douglas Woody Woodsum**, from Smithfield, has won an Avery Hopwood Award and the Bread Loaf Poetry Prize. He recently published the volume *The Lawns of Lobstermen.*

ACKNOWLEDGMENTS

Linda Aldrich: "Valentine" and "After Another Difficult Week" copyright © 2012 Linda Aldrich. Reprinted from *March and Mad Women*, Cherry Grove Collections, 2012, by permission of Linda Aldrich.

Richard Aldridge: "Moth at My Window" copyright © 1980 by Richard Aldridge. Reprinted from *Red Pine, Black Ash*, Thorndike Press, 1980, by permission of the Estate of Richard Aldridge. "The Red and Green Cement Truck" copyright © 2001 by Richard Aldridge. Reprinted from *The Poems of Richard Aldridge,* 2001, by permission of Josephine Haskell Aldridge.

Lynn Ascrizzi: "New England Asters" and "Ants" copyright by Lynn Ascrizzi. Reprinted from *Puckerbrush Review*, Puckerbrush Press Inc., by permission of Sandy Phippen and Lynn Ascizzi.

Carol Willette Bachofner: "Loon Return" copyright © 2011 by Carol Willette Bachofner. Reprinted from *I Write in the Greenhouse,* Front Porch Books, 2011, by permission of Carol Willette Bachofner. "Unknown Algonquin Females" copyright © 2009 by Carol Willette Bachofner. Reprinted from *Crab Orchard Review,* 2009, by permission of Carol Willette Bachofner.

Kate Barnes: "Peaches," "April and Then May," "Another Full Moon," and "Inside the Stone" copyright © 1994 by David R. Godine. Reprinted from *Where the Deer Were,* David R. Godine, 1994, by permission of David R. Godine. "In the Pasture" copyright © 2008 Kate Barnes. Reprinted from *Agreeable Friends: Contemporary Animal Poetry,* Moon Pie Press, 2008, by permission of Kate Barnes.

Christian Barter: "The School Bus" copyright © Christian Barter. Reprinted from *The Singers I Prefer*, CavanKerry Press Ltd., 2005, by permission of Christian Barter.

Richard Blanco: "When I was a Little Cuban Boy" copyright © 2005 Richard Blanco. Reprinted from *Directions to the Beach of the Dead,* The University of Arizona Press, 2005, by permission of Richard Blanco. "Burning in the Rain," "My Father, My Hands," and "Thicker Than Country" copyright © 2012 by Richard Blanco. Reprinted from *Looking for the Gulf Motel,* University of Pittsburgh Press, 2012, by permission of Richard Blanco.

Louise Bogan: "Night," "Musician," "Question in a Field," "To an Artist, To Take Heart," and "The Dragonfly" copyright © 1968 by Louise Bogan. Reprinted from *The Blue Estuaries: Poems: 1923–1968,* Farrar Straus and Giroux, New York, 1968, by permission of Farrar, Straus and Giroux.

Ted Bookey: "The Power of It" copyright © 2005 by Ted Bookey. Reprinted from *A Moxie and a Moon Pie: The Best of Moon Pie Press,* Volume 1, Moon Pie Press, 2005, by permission of Ted Bookey.

Philip Booth: "Old" and "United States" copyright © 1990 by Philip Booth. Reprinted from *Selves,* Penguin Publishing, 1990, by permission of Viking Penguin, a division of Penguin Group (USA) Inc. "Sixty" and "Fog-Talk" copyright © 1999 by Philip Booth. Reprinted from *Lifelines,* Penguin Publishing, 1999, by permission of Viking Penguin, a division of Penguin Group (USA) Inc.

Henry Braun: "Growing Lettuce," from "Under Mount Blue," and "The Great Rock in the Woods" copyright © 2006 by Henry Braun. Reprinted from *Loyalty: New and Selected Poems,* Off the Grid Press, 2006, by permission of Henry Braun.

Marcia F. Brown: "Freeze Frame," "Valentines," and "Geography" copyright © 2010 Marcia F. Brown. Reprinted from *What on Earth*, Moon Pie Press, 2010, by permission of Marcia F. Brown.

Sharon Bray: "1940" copyright © 2008 by Sharon Bray. Reprinted from *A Rump-Sprung Chair and a One-Eyed Cat*, Black Dog Press, 2008, by permission of Sharon Bray, Gerald George, and the Salt Coast Sages.

Bob Brooks: "Regret" and "Snap" copyright © 2011 by Bob Brooks. Reprinted from *Unguarded Crossing,* Antrim House, 2011, by permission of Bob Brooks.

Linda Buckmaster: "Sudden Death" and "January" copyright © 2007 by Linda Buckmaster. Reprinted from *Heart Song & Other Legacies*, Illuminated Sea Press, 2007, by permission of Linda Buckmaster.

Thomas Carper: "Roses," "Nobody at Treblinka," and "The Solemn Son" copyright © 1991 by Thomas Carper. Reprinted from *Fiddle Lane*, John Hopkins University Press, 1991, by permission of Thomas Carper. "Her Harvest" copyright © 2011 Thomas Carper. Reprinted from *Creators*, author manuscript edition, by permission of Thomas Carper.

Robert M. Chute: "Driving Down East" copyright © 2010 by Robert M. Chute. Reprinted from *Maine Taproot*, Encircle Publications, 2010, by permission of Robert M. Chute. "Faith" copyright © 2012 Robert M. Chute. Reprinted from *Favorites From the First Fifteen Years*, Encircle Publications LLC, 2012, by permission of Robert M. Chute.

Elizabeth Coatsworth: "Night Wind in Spring" and " Lost Graveyards" copyright © 1968 by Elizabeth Coatsworth. Reprinted from *Down Half the World*, Macmillan, 1968, by permission of Kate Barnes. "From Cadillac Mountain" copyright © 2006 Elizabeth Coatsworth. Reprinted from *The Maine Poets: An Anthology of Verse*, Down East Books, 2006, by permission of the Estate of Catherine Beston Barnes. "July Storm" copyright © 1963 Elizabeth Coatsworth. Reprinted from *Down East* magazine, July 1963, by permission of Estate of Catherine Beston Barnes.

Robert P. Tristram Coffin: "Winter Friends" and "Brothers" copyright © 1948 by Robert P. Tristram Coffin. Reprinted from *Collected Poems of Robert P. Tristram Coffin*, The Macmillan Company, American Book - Stratford Press, 1948, by permission of June Coffin.

Donald Crane: "Divorce" copyright © 2008 by Donald Crane. Reprinted from *Puckerbrush Review*, Winter/Spring 2008, Puckerbrush Press, 2008, by permission of Donald Crane.

Marnie Reed Crowell: "Three Poems About Birds" copyright © 2011 Marnie Reed Crowell. Reprinted from *A Sky of Birds,* Three-half Press, 2011, by permission of Marnie Reed Crowell.

Jay Davis: "Potatoes" copyright © 2004 by Jay Davis. Reprinted from *Whispers, Cries, and Tantrums,* Moon Pie Press, 2004, by permission of Jay Davis.

Theodore Enslin: "The Glass Harmonica" copyright © 1958 by Theodore Enslin. Reprinted from *Then and Now,* National Poetry Foundation Press, 1999, by permission of Theodore Enslin. "Vespers" Copyright 1994 by Theodore Enslin. Reprinted from *The Quotable Moose: A Contemporary Maine Reader,* University Press of New England, 1994.

Annie Farnsworth: "Spaghetti Western Days" copyright © 2006 by Annie Farnsworth. Reprinted from *Angel of the Heavenly Tailgate,* Moon Pie Press, 2006, by permission of Annie Farnsworth. "For the Falling Man" copyright © 2001 by Annie Farnsworth. Reprinted from *Bodies of Water, Bodies of Light,* Sheltering Pine Press, 2001, by permission of Annie Farnsworth.

Gibson Fay-LeBlanc: "The Nots," "One of the Dummies at Night," and "Worry Bone" copyright © 2012 Gibson Fay-LeBlanc. Reprinted from *Death of a Ventriloquist,* University of North Texas Press, by permission of Gibson Fay-LeBlanc.

Annie Finch: "Shell" copyright © 2012 Annie Finch. Reprinted from *The Voice Was the Sea,* The Center for the Study of Place, Inc., 2012, by permission of Annie Finch.

Marta Rijn Finch: "The Poet" copyright © 2011 by Marta Rijn Finch. Reprinted from *A Solitary Piper,* Encircle Publications, 2011, by permission of Marta Rijn Finch.

Rachel Contreni Flynn: "Hunger for Something Easier" and "Coydog" copyright © 2010 Rachel Contreni Flynn. Reprinted from *Tongue,* Red Hen Press, 2010, by permission of Rachel Contreni Flynn. "On Wanting Only One Thing" and "Gold Stars" copyright © 2005 Rachel Contreni Flynn. Reprinted from *Ice, Mouth, Song,* Tupelo Press, 2005, by permission of Rachel Contreni Flynn.

Richard Foerster: "Garden Spider" copyright © 2002 by Richard Foerster. Reprinted from *Double Going,* BOA Editions, Ltd., 2005, by permission of Richard Foerster. "Fiddleheads" copyright © 1998 by Richard Foerster. Reprinted from *Trillium*, BOA Editions, Ltd., 1998, by permission of Richard Foerster. "At the Birdfeeder" copyright © 2010 Richard Foerster. Reprinted from *Penetralia*, Texas Review Press, 2010, by permission of Richard Foerster.

Elizabeth W. Garber: "Feasting" copyright © 2004 by Elizabeth W. Garber. Reprinted from *Pierced by the Seasons,* The Illuminated Sea Press, 2004, by permission of Elizabeth W. Garber. "Island Transport" and "The Man Who Looked Like Elvis" copyright © 2011 Elizabeth Garber. Reprinted from *True Affections: Poems from a Small Town*, The Illuminated Sea Press, 2011, by permission of Elizabeth Garber.

Gerald George: "Rained Out" copyright © 2008 by Gerald George. Reprinted from *A Rump-Sprung Chair and a One-Eyed Cat*, Black Dog Press, 2008, by permission of Gerald George, Sharon Bray, and the Salt Coast Sages.

Kimberly Cloutier Green: "About Bees Is What I Say Aloud When You Ask What I'm Thinking" and "What Now, Praying?" copyright © 2013 Kimberly Cloutier Green. Reprinted from *The Next Hunger*, Bauhan Publishing, 2013, by permission of Kimberly Cloutier Green.

Megan Grumbling: "Rock Maples" copyright © 2006 Megan Grumbling. Reprinted from the *Southern Review*, by permission of Megan Grumbling. "Some Kind of Hunter" copyright © 2006 Megan Grumbling. Reprinted from *Poetry* magazine, 2006, by permission of Megan Grumbling.

Bruce Guernsey: "The Dump Pickers," "The Present," and "The Lady and the Tramp" copyright © 2012 by Bruce Guernsey. Reprinted from *From Rain: Poems 1970–2010*, Ecco Qua Press, 2012, by permission of Bruce Guernsey. "Night Patrol" and "The Hands" copyright © 2004 by Water Press & Media. Reprinted from *The Lost Brigade,* Water Press & Media, 2004, by permission of Water Press & Media.

Ruth F. Guillard: "Spring Thaw" copyright © 2011 by Ruth F. Guillard: Reprinted from *Transitions,* Adagio Press, 2011, by permission of Ruth F. Guillard.

Peter Harris: "The Net" copyright © 1999 by Peter Harris. Reprinted from *The Atlantic*. 1999, by permission of Peter Harris.

Nancy A. Henry: "From the Toy Box" copyright © 2002 by Nancy A. Henry. Reprinted from *SARX*, Moon Pie Press, 2010, by permission of Nancy A. Henry. "Sixty-five Degrees" copyright © 2010 Nancy A. Henry. Reprinted from *Favorites from the First Fifteen Years*, Encircle Publications, 2010, by permission of Nancy A. Henry.

Claire Hersom: "October Moon" copyright © 2008 Claire Hersom. Reprinted from *Drowning: A Poetic Memoir,* Moon Pie Press, 2008, by permission of Claire Hersom.

Preston H. Hood: "Cullen: Four Days Old, Waking" copyright © 2011 by Preston H. Hood. Reprinted from *The Hallelujah of Listening,* Červená Barva Press, 2011, by permission of Preston H. Hood.

Constance Hunting: "The Pet" copyright © 2000 Constance Hunting. Reprinted from *Natural Things: Collected Poems 1969-1998,* The National Poetry Foundation, 2000, by permission of Sam Hunting.

Sheila Gray Jordan: "The Man Who Likes Cows" and "Salt and Pepper" copyright © 1995 by Sheila Gray Jordan. Reprinted from *The China in the Sea*, Signal Books, 1995, by permission of Sheila Gray Jordan. "In Nightgowns" copyright © 2010 by Sheila Gray Jordan. Reprinted from *Winter Wall*, Stone Sleep Books, 2010, by permission of Sheila Gray Jordan.

Stuart Kestenbaum: "Essence," "The Light," and "Laughter" copyright © 2003 by Stuart Kestenbaum. Reprinted from *House of Thanksgiving,* Deerbrook Editions, 2003, by permission of Stuart Kestenbaum. "Mr. Fix-It" and "April Prayer" copyright © 2007 by Stuart Kestenbaum. Reprinted from *Prayers & Run-on Sentences,* Deerbrook Editions, 2007, by permission of Stuart Kestenbaum. "Prayer for Joy" copyright © 2014 Stuart Kestenbaum. Reprinted from *Only Now,* Deerbrook Editions, 2014, by permission of Stuart Kestenbaum. "Starting the Subaru at Five Below" copyright © 2010 Stuart Kestenbaum. Reprinted from *Maine in Four Seasons,* Down East Books, 2010, by permission of Stuart Kestenbaum.

Susan Deborah King: "Watermelon," "Frenchboro," and "Up with Fishermen and Birds" copyright © 2010 by Susan Deborah King. Reprinted from *Bog Orchids: Island Poems,* The Island Institute, 2010, by permission of Susan Deborah King.

Gary Lawless: "Some Clear Night" and "Which World" copyright © 1998 by Gary Lawless. Reprinted from *Caribouddhism*, Blackberry Books, 1998, by permission of Gary Lawless. "Listening for Loons" copyright © Gary Lawless. Reprinted from *Listening for Loons*, by permission of Gary Lawless.

Carl Little: "Zones of Peeper" copyright © 2009 by Carl Little. Reprinted from *Down East* magazine, March 2009, by permission of Carl Little. "Last Writes" copyright © 2010 by Carl Little. Reprinted from *Off the Coast*, Fall 2010, by permission of Carl Little. "Young Pine" copyright © 2010 Carl Little. Reprinted from *Maine in Four Seasons*, Down East Books, 2010, by permission of Carl Little. "Glacial Erotic" copyright © 2006 Carl Little. Reprinted from *Ocean Drinker: New and Selected Poems,* Deerbrook Editions, 2006, by permission of Carl Little.

Kristen Lindquist: "Transportation" copyright © 2001 by Kristen Lindquist. Reprinted from *Invocation to the Birds*, Oyster River Press, 2001, by permission of Kristen Lindquist.

Carolyn Locke: "Regeneration" copyright © 2010 by Carolyn Locke. Reprinted from *Always this Falling,* Maine Authors Publishing, 2010, by permission of Carolyn Locke.

Michael Macklin: "Resurrection" copyright © 2004 by Michael Macklin. Reprinted from *A Moxie and A Moon Pie: The Best of Moon Pie Press,* Moon Pie Press, 2005, by permission of Michael Macklin.

Bob MacLaughlin: "Ball Smacks Mouth, Splits Lip" copyright © 2011 by Bob MacLaughlin. Reprinted from *Faulty Wiring: the Alzheimer's Poems and Other Memories*, Moon Pie Press, 2001, by permission of Bob MacLaughlin.

Mekeel McBride: "The Goldfish," "Where Inspiration Has Learned a Thing or Two," "Mockingbird," "Strauss and the Cows of Ireland," and "No Child of Earthly Kitchens" copyright © 2006 by Mekeel McBride. Reprinted from *Dog Star Delicatessen,* Carnegie Mellon University Press, 2006, by permission of Mekeel McBride. "A Little Bit of Timely Advice" and "The Pain Sweepstakes" copyright © 1995 by Mekeel McBride. Reprinted from *Wind of the White Dresses*, Carnegie Mellon University Press, 1995, by permission of Mekeel McBride.

Elizabeth McFarland: "Feed My Birds" copyright © 1984 by Elizabeth McFarland. Reprinted from *Over the Summer Water*, Orchises Press, 2008, by permission of Daniel G. Hoffman, Trustee, Estate of Elizabeth McFarland Hoffman.

Robin Merrill: "Out Here" and "Thousand Dollar Thumbs" copyright © 2005 by Robin Merrill. Reprinted from *Laundry and Stories,* Moon Pie Press, 2005, by permission of Robin Merrill.

Edna St. Vincent Millay: "Love Is Not All: It Is Not Meat Nor Drink," "To Jesus on His Birthday," and "Hearing Your Words, and Not a Word Among Them" copyright © 1931, 1958 by Edna St. Vincent Millay and Norma Millay Ellis. Reprinted by permission of Holly Peppe, Literary Executor, The Millay Society.

Leslie Moore: "Coyotes" copyright © 2013 Leslie Moore. Reprinted from *Coyote Lives in Maine,* Geri Vistein, by permission of Leslie Moore. "To a Garden Spider" copyright © 1992 Leslie Moore. Reprinted from *English Journal*, National Council of English Teachers, April 1992, by permission of Leslie Moore. "After the Splash" copyright © 2014 Leslie Moore. Reprinted by permission of Leslie Moore.

Thomas R. Moore: "Her Telling" and "The Plymouth on Ice" copyright © 2010 by Thomas R. Moore. Reprinted from *The Bolt-Cutters,* Fort Hemlock Press, 2010, by permission of Thomas R. Moore. "Chick Magnets" and "Summer Episcopalians" copyright © 2012 Thomas R. Moore. Reprinted from *Chet Sawing*, Fort Hemlock Press, 2012, by permission of Thomas R. Moore.

David Moreau: "Salt to the Brain" copyright © 2005 by David Moreau. Reprinted from *A Moxie and a Moon Pie: The Best of Moon Pie Press,* Volume 1, Moon Pie Press, 2005, by permission of David Moreau.

Dave Morrison: "Closing Time" and "He Sees the Future" copyright

© 2011 by Dave Morrison. Reprinted from *Clubland,* Fighting Cock Press, 2011, by permission of Dave Morrison.

Paul Nelson: "Night Out" copyright © 1982 Paul Nelson. Reprinted from *Days Off*, 1982, by permission of Paul Nelson.

Edward Nobles: "Sentences" copyright © 2000 by Edward Nobles. Reprinted from *The Bluestone Walk*, Persea Books, 2000, by permission of Edward Nobles. "Where He Went" copyright © 2010 by Edward Nobles.

Mihku Paul: "Mother Tongue" copyright © 2012 Mihku Paul. Reprinted from *20th Century PowWow Playland,* Bowman Books, 2012, by permission of Mihku Paul.

Alice Persons: "Mud Season" copyright © 2005 by Alice Persons. Reprinted from *A Moxie and a Moon Pie: The Best of Moon Pie Press,* Volume 1, Moon Pie Press, 2005, by permission of Alice Persons. "Stealing Lilacs" copyright © 2004 by Alice Persons. Reprinted from *Never Say Never,* Moon Pie Press, 2004, by permission of Alice Persons. "The Man in Front of You" copyright © 2011 Alice N. Persons. Reprinted from *Thank Your Lucky Stars,* Moon Pie Press, 2011, by permission of Alice Persons. "Why I Have a Crush on You, UPS Man" copyright © 2007 Alice N. Persons. Reprinted from *Don't Be A Stranger,* Sheltering Pines Press, 2007, by permission of Alice N. Persons.

Dawn Potter: "After Twenty Years" and "Dog in Winter" copyright © 2014 Dawn Potter. Reprinted from *Same Old Story,* Cavankerry Press, 2014, by permission of Dawn Potter.

Gary Rainford: "Miss Shrew" copyright © 2014 Gary Rainford. Reprinted from Salty Liquor, North Country Press, 2014, by permission of Gary Rainford.

Patricia Smith Ranzoni: "Housekeeping of a Kind" copyright ©

1995 by Patricia Ranzoni. Reprinted from *Claiming*, Puckerbrush Press, 1995, by permission of Patricia Ranzoni. "If You Should Die Before I Do" and "The Old Gross Place" copyright © 2000 by Patricia Ranzoni. Reprinted from *Settling*, Puckerbrush Press, 2000, by permission of Patricia Ranzoni. "September Staying" copyright © Patricia Ranzoni. Reprinted from *Maine in Four Seasons*, Down East Books, 2010, by permission of Patricia Ranzoni.

Edward J. Rielly: "Hands Reaching" and "The Lost Seed" copyright © 2005 by Edward J. Rielly. Reprinted from *Ways of Looking: Poems of the Farm,* Moon Pie Press, 2005, by permission of Edward J. Rielly. "Old Whitman Loved Baseball" and "Homering Among the Pines" copyright © 2007 Edward J. Reilly. Reprinted from *Old Whitman Loved Baseball and Other Baseball Poems,* Moon Pie Press, 2007, by permission of Edward J. Reilly.

Kenneth Rosen: "The Last Lamplighters" and "The Alligator's Hum" copyright © 2003 by Kenneth Rosen. Reprinted from *The Origins of Tragedy & Other Poems*, CavanKerry Press, 2003, by permission of Kenneth Rosen.

Ira Sadoff: "My Mother's Funeral" copyright © 1998 by Ira Sadoff. Reprinted from *Grazing: Poems,* University of Illinois Press, 1998, by permission of Ira Sadoff.

Marija Sanderling: "Free Agent" copyright © 2010 by Marija Sanderling. Reprinted from *Maine Taproot*, Encircle Publications, 2010, by permission of Marija Sanderling.

May Sarton: "Death and the Turtle," "A Parrot," and "The Geese" copyright © 1993, 1988, 1984, 1980, 1974 by May Sarton. Reprinted from *Collected Poems: 1930-1993,* W. W. Norton & Company, Inc., by permission of W. W. Norton & Company, Inc.

Tom Sexton: "Porcupine" copyright © 2009 by Tom Sexton. Reprinted from *For the Sake of the Light,* University of Alaska Press,

2009, by permission of Tom Sexton. "Washington County, Maine" and "By Passamaquoddy Bay" copyright © 2011 by Tom Sexton. Reprinted from *I Think Again of Those Ancient Chinese Poets,* University of Alaska Press, 2011, by permission of Tom Sexton. "Sardine Packer" and "The Granite Stoop" copyright © 2012 Tom Sexton. Reprinted from *Bridge Street at Dusk*, Loom Press, 2012, by permission of Tom Sexton. "Crossing the Blueberry Barrens" copyright © 2004 Tom Sexton. Reprinted from the *Hudson Review*, 2004, by permission of Tom Sexton.

J. Barrie Shepherd: "The Silent Seers" copyright ©2012 J. Barrie Shepherd. Reprinted from *Between Mirage and Miracle*, Wipf and Stock Press, 2012, by permission of the publisher.

Betsy Sholl: "Gulls in Wind" copyright © 2003 by Betsy Sholl. Reprinted from the *Maine Times*, 2003, by permission of Betsy Sholl. "To the Infinitesimal" and "Doing Time" copyright © 2009 by Betsy Sholl. Reprinted from *Rough Cradle*, Alice James Books, 2009, by permission of Alice James Books, Farmington, Maine. "Alms" copyright © 2014 Betsy Sholl. Reprinted from *Otherwise Unseeable*, University of Wisconsin Press, 2014, by permission of Betsy Sholl.

Weslea Sidon: "Closure" copyright © 2014 Weslea Sidon. Reprinted from *The Fool Sings,* Rain Chain Press, 2014, by permission of Weslea Sidon.

Robert Siegel: "How to Catch a Poem," "Mantis," "Nude," "Airfield," "Peonies," "Shopping Together," and "A Notable Failure" copyright © 2001 by Robert Siegel. Reprinted from *A Pentecost of Finches: New and Selected Poems,* Paraclete Press, 2006, by permission of Robert Siegel.

David Sloan: "Stunned" copyright © 2013 David Sloan. Reprinted from *The Irresistible In-Between,* Deerbrook Editions, 2013, by permission of David Sloan.

Pam Burr Smith: "Sandwiches" copyright © 2011 by Pam Burr Smith. Reprinted from *Heaven Jumping Woman*, Moon Pie Press, 2011, by permission of Pam Burr Smith.

Bruce Spang: "Humane Society" copyright © 2002 by Bruce Spang. Reprinted from *The Knot*, Snowdrift Press, 2002, by permission of Bruce Spang.

Martin Steingesser: "Today the Traffic Signals All Changed for Me," "Mom Gets in One of My Poems," and "Fishing" copyright © 2012 by Martin Steingesser. Reprinted from *Brothers of Morning,* Deerbrook Editions, 2012, by permission of Martin Steingesser. "Between Stars" copyright © 2013 Martin Steingesser. Reprinted from *Words & Images*, 2013, by permission of Martin Steingesser.

Candice Stover: "Appointment" and "Briefly, Enough" copyright © 2007 Candice Stover. Reprinted from *Poems from the Pond*, Deerbrook Editions, 2007, by permission of Candice Stover.

John Tagliabue: "What Position Do They and We Assume in the Encapsulated Stillness?" copyright © 1997 by John Tagliabue. Reprinted from *New and Selected Poems: 1942–1997*, National Poetry Foundation Press, 1997, by permission of the estate of John Tagliabue.

Haines Sprunt Tate: "Balloon" and "Keepsake" copyright © 2013 by the estate of Isabelle Haines Sprunt Tate. Reprinted from *Strata and Other Poems,* Ghost Leaf Press, 2013 (available from ondemandbooks.com), by permission of Duncan Tate.

Ellen M. Taylor: "Spring Cleaning," "Hummingbird," and "Hen" copyright © 2009 by Ellen M. Taylor. Reprinted from *Floating,* Moon Pie Press, 2009, by permission of Ellen M. Taylor.

Jim Glenn Thatcher: "Understory" copyright © 2008 by Jim Glenn Thatcher. Reprinted from *The Ur-Word*, Moon Pie Press, 2008, by permission of Jim Glenn Thatcher.

Jeffrey Thomson: "El Café a la Esquina de Agua y Vida, Seville" copyright © 2014 by Jeffrey Thomson. Reprinted from *Connotation Press*, 2014, by permission of Jeffrey Thomson.

Elizabeth Tibbetts: "Eighty-five," "Coming Home," "Snow," and "Saint of Returnables" copyright © 2002 by Elizabeth Tibbetts. Reprinted from *In the Well*, Bluestem Press at Emporia State University, 2002, by permission of Elizabeth Tibbetts.

Mariana S. Tupper: "My Hairy Legs" copyright © 2006 by Mariana S. Tupper. Reprinted from *Off the Coast*, May 2006, Resolute Bear Press, by permission of Mariana S. Tupper. "Magic Show" copyright © 2002 by Mariana Tupper. Reprinted from *A Sense of Place, Collected Maine Poems*, Bay River Press, 2002, by permission of Mariana S. Tupper.

Lewis Turco: "The Street" and "The Habitation" copyright © 2007 by Lewis Turco. Reprinted from *Fearful Pleasures: The Complete Poems of Lewis Turco 1959–2007*, Star Cloud Press, 2007, by permission of Lewis Turco.

George V. Van Deventer: "Early Morning Trumpet" copyright © 1988 by George V. Van Deventer. Printed by permission George V. Van Deventer.

David Walker: "The Crossing" copyright © 1976 by the Rector and Visitors of the University of Virginia. Reprinted from *Moving Out,* University Press of Virginia, 1976, by permission of Rector and Visitors of the University of Virginia. "A Prayer, A Welcome," copyright © 1976 by David Walker. Reprinted from *The Maine Poets,* Down East Books, 2003, by permission of Down East Books.

Bruce Willard: "Elegy for the Stepfather" copyright © 2013 Bruce Willard. Reprinted from *Holding Ground*, Four Way Books, 2013, by permission of Four Way Books, all rights reserved.

Sarah Woolf-Wade: "Making the Turn" and "They All Come Back" copyright © 2008 by Sarah Jane Woolf-Wade. Reprinted from *Down the Bristol Road*, Snow Drift Press, 2008, by permission of Sarah Jane Woolf-Wade.

Douglas Woody Woodsum: "Spooked Moose" copyright © 2007 by Douglas Woodsum. Reprinted from *Down East* magazine, Down East Enterprise, Inc., October 2007, by permission of Douglas Woodsum. "Splitting Wood in Winter" copyright © 2010 Douglas Woodsum. Reprinted from *The Lawns of Lobsterman,* Moon Pie Press, by permission of Douglas Woodsum.

Called by poet Philip Levine one of the great storytellers of contemporary poetry, **Wesley McNair** is the author of more than twenty books, including his recent titles, *Late Wonders: New and Selected Poems, Dwellers in the House of the Lord,* and *The Unfastening.* He has twice been invited by the Library of Congress to read his poetry, and has won the Robert Frost and Theodore Roethke Prizes, grants from the Fulbright and Guggenheim Foundations, two Rockefeller Fellowships, two grants in poetry from the National Endowment for the Arts, and the Sarah Josepha Hale Medal for his "distinguished contribution to the world of letters." McNair has served five times on the jury for the Pulitzer Prize in Poetry. In 2006 he was selected for a United States Artist Fellowship as one of America's finest living artists. He was Maine's Poet Laureate from 2011 to 2016.